A HARVEST OF CHAFF.

BY

OWEN SEAMAN,

Author of
"*Borrowed Plumes,*" "*In Cap and Bells,*"
"*The Battle of the Bays,*" *&c.*

SECOND EDITION.

LONDON :

ARCHIBALD CONSTABLE & CO., LTD.

1907.

BRADBURY, AGNEW, & CO. LD., PRINTERS,
LONDON AND TONBRIDGE.

WITH the exception of the lines to Mr. Austin Dobson, all these verses have appeared in *Punch*, and for permission to republish them I have to thank the courtesy of Messrs. Bradbury and Agnew. To a former collection, "In Cap and Bells," I appended a few memorial verses, by right of the fool's prerogative of being serious at times; so here, to this "harvest of chaff," I have added a few grains of memory's garnering. Under this image there is no implication that these lines, prompted by solemn occasion, are to be counted as good grain; simply I want to make apology for their inclusion in a book with so vacant a title.

O. S.

CONTENTS.

LINES IN MEMORIAM.

A HARVEST OF CHAFF.

MUSCULAR WOMEN.

I.—THE YELLOW SHIN-PADS.

[After William Morris's *The Gilliflower of Gold*.]

A PAIR of leggings, largest size,
I wore to-day with bloomer guise,
And won the local Hockey Prize.
   Hah! hah! les belles jaunes jambières!

Your hands had tied them on for me,
Fair lord, and righteous referee,
Above my crushers, daintily.
   Hah! hah! les belles jaunes jambières!

However hard Miss Jones might hit,
Though on my legs the missile lit,
I felt it not one little bit.
   Hah! hah! les belles jaunes jambières!

And when my stick in fragments flew,
Bringing to earth their only Blue,
I smiled aloud and looked at you.
   Hah! hah! les belles jaunes jambières!

B

But ere her ribs had ceased to shake
I took another stick and brake
Her livid thumb for my love's sake.
Hah! hah! les belles jaunes jambières!

My golden hair was getting loose,
Yet fell I out on that excuse?
Not so; I dribbled like the deuce.
Hah! hah! les belles jaunes jambières!

And when the half-fought fight was stayed
I scorned the lemon's feeble aid
And quaffed a gin-and-gingerade.
Hah! hah! les belles jaunes jambières!

Then like a fiery steed in stall
I scarce could wait the whistle's call,
But chafed to be upon the ball.
Hah! hah! les belles jaunes jambières!

Miss Brown (of Bucks) against me drew;
She wore a shirt of purple hue;
Our score was one, and theirs was two.
Hah! hah! les belles jaunes jambières!

Red-cheeked I charged this bounding half,
And as I hooked her by the calf
I heard your low elusive laugh.
Hah! hah! les belles jaunes jambières!

I reached the goal; in ruthless wise
I caught the warder 'twixt the eyes,
And so achieved to equalise.
Hah! hah! les belles jaunes jambières!

Much heated, I began to think
That I should prematurely sink
For need of just another drink.
   Hah ! hah ! les belles jaunes jambières !

And then I thought of your dear knee
Bent as you bound my pads for me
Above my crushers daintily.
   Hah ! hah ! les belles jaunes jambières !

Whew ! how the meeting sticks went whack !
Yea, o'er the field I heard the crack
Of stitches giving down the back.
   Hah ! hah ! les belles jaunes jambières !

One minute still ! My teeth were set ;
I and the stout custodian met ;
The ball (and she) went through the net !
   Hah ! hah ! les belles jaunes jambières !

And as with face profusely hot
(*Les belles ! les belles !*) I faltered not,
But reached and took the Challenge-pot,
   (*Hah ! hah ! les belles jaunes jambières !*)

I saw again your supple knee
Bent as you bound my pads for me,
My yellow shin-pads, daintily.
   Hah ! hah ! les belles jaunes jambières !

II.—LUCY GRAY.

[After Wordsworth]

WELL I remember Lucy Gray
  In skirt of two-some cut,
For on the links one Medal day
  I boshed her winning put.

And often through an oversight,
  When she was still alive,
My head delayed her pellet's flight
  And spoilt a spanking drive.

Hard by a sporting course she kept,
  All sandy from the sea;
No keener artist ever stepped
  Upon a human tee.

You still may hear strong men at play
  Blaspheming on the green,
But I regret that Lucy Gray
  Will never more be seen.

" My child, your tastes are very low !
  They hurt your mother's heart ;
O take your sampler up and sew,
  Or bake a little tart ! "

" That, mother, I will never do !
  Last night I lay and dreamt
I'd do ' The Pit ' to-day in two,
  Or die in the attempt."

The mother gave her child the look
  Which Lucy could not stand ;
At once she said " Ta-ta ! " and took
  Her weapons in her hand.

Blithe as the young opossum flits,
  With many a sturdy hack
She cut the living turf in bits,
  And failed to put it back.

A blizzard blew at 4.15,
  The sky was black as coal ;
Her ball was on the eighteenth green,
  But never in the hole.

Her loving parents, when they found
  She came not home to tea,
Sought for her round the solid ground,
  And slightly out to sea.

The wind blew landward, rude and raw ;
  'Twas time to be in bed,
When on the eighteenth tee they saw
  Poor Lucy's bulger's head.

" A foozled drive ! " the father cried ;
  " Pray heaven she did not swear ! "
But close at hand the mother spied
  Great hunks of Lucy's hair.

Then, by the bull's-eye lantern's glow,
  Advancing from the tee
They found a shaft that lay as though
  Snapped clean across the knee.

Later, they struck the bunker's edge
    That blocked the eighteenth hole;
And there they marked below the ledge
    Signs of a hob-nailed sole!

Across "The Pit" they pounded hard
    On these abnormal prints;
While niblick-furrows, every yard,
    Provided further hints.

And now in drift and driving sleet
    They lost, with many a groan,
The speaking trace of Lucy's feet,
    And scarce could lift their own.

At last, when both had long gone lame
    And fairly spent their force,
Up to their eyes in sand they came
    On Lucy's bunkered corse!

They found her ball, at rise of sun,
    Dead, too, against the hole;
It was the final shot but one
    Had freed the panting soul!

Yet have I known of some who swore
    The child might yet be seen;
They still could hear her thundering "Fore!"
    Shatter the eighteenth green.

Then such have taken wings and fled,
    Nor ever looked behind;
Fearing to see her bulger-head
    Come whistling down the wind.

III.—" THE GUINEAS ; "

OR, HOW THEY BROUGHT THE GOOD NEWS FROM NEWMARKET TO GIRTON.

[After Robert Browning.]

I.

I SWUNG to the saddle, and Doris, and she ;
I pedalled, Joan pedalled, we pedalled all
    three ;
" Well done ! " yelled the paddock ; the Varsity
    yelled ;
" Done ! " echoed the bookie whose bullion I
    held ;
As with bells hard a-ringing and horns going
    Toot !
We debouched from the Ring on the Bottisham
    route.

II.

Conversation was none ; we were nursing our
    breath,
As we rode, knee to knee, in the silence of death ;
Not a lurch was observed, not a wobble was felt,
When I hitched up my bloomers and tightened
    my belt ;
Then stooped to the wind with my back like a
    bow,
And my gear at a hundred-and-sixty or so.

III.

Our way at Quywater was queered by a cow,
But we stove in her haunches, I never knew
    how;
At Teversham Joan had a touch of the cramp,
Her nose being rather too near to her lamp;
And at Barnwell, in dodging a beast of a mule,
We were into the ruck of a primary school.

IV.

Three moribund infants lay out in our wake
As we panted "So long!"—for appearance's
    sake;
Some sort of a Nemesis chased us in carts,
But we scorched at our bravest and swallowed
    our hearts;
King's turrets in sight! we were over the worst,
When the Dunlop of Joan met a bottle and
    burst!

V.

I omit to record the expressions she used, ·
With a list of the various parties accused;
We remarked on her luck, but declined to alight,
Though our hubs were red-hot and our bearings
    were tight;
So we splashed through a puddle and spurted
    again
Past Midsummer Common and into the Lane.

VI.

To the right with a skid at the gutter we raced;
By the Union a couple of cabs were displaced;
My off-knicker was rent and the knee showing
    through,
But we flattened our chests on the handles, and
    flew;
We were flush with the bridge, we were flying
    the Cam,
When Doris was heard to say something like
    "Dear me!"

VII.

She was right—as she proved to me, later, in
    bed—
For her axle had split, and the same with her head;
Though I guessed she had gone to her ultimate
    sleep,
Yet I shouted a "Righto!" and shot up the
    steep;
For I still had to tackle the best of a league,
And my treadles were showing a trace of fatigue.

VIII.

I was up to the Castle and clear of the town,
With my tongue hanging out and my hair coming
    down;
Then I rose in my seat and went out of my mind
To the clink of our winnings that waggled behind;

Clapped my boots, waived my brake, ran amok
    though a dog,
Till at last into Girton I fell like a log.

IX.

Of the rest I remember a roar of applause
As I lay with a splinter of spoke in my jaws;
There was whiskey for one and an oil-bath for two,
Which they said, very frankly, was only our due,
Who had broken the record, and several teeth,
In conveying their yellow-boys home from the
    Heath.

IV.—THE VICAR'S DAUGHTER.

[A fragment, after Tennyson.]

*   *   *   *

So sit and sing it, if you please,
  Sing it, my Alice, while I lean
Backward against your brawny knees,
  Beside the mown grass freshly green;
The old sweet scent assails my nose
  Here where I nursed those early hopes,
Watching you whack my helpless slows
  Far-humming to the rounded ropes.

Alice sings :
  "It is the Vicar's daughter,
    And her arm has grown so stout
  That I would be the willow
    With which she swipes about;

And I would hardly wince a bit
Although I ultimately split.

" And I would be the bulwark
    Upon her stalwart, stalwart shin,
And all day long to shield her
    While her eye was getting in ;
And help her not to feel too sore
When obviously ' limb before.'

" And I would be the gauntlet
    Upon her fairy finger-tips,
To guard her knotted knuckles
    When steering through the slips ;
And bear the language of my love
When people bowled her off her glove.

" Is she the demon trundler ?
    I'd be the bounding, bounding sphere,
Flung high and hard at random
    About the batsman's ear ;
And I would throb with happy throes,
Letting her pitch me where she chose."

The gentleman resumes :
A trifle, but the best I could !
    Not tricked, I own, with gawds of art ;
But you, you found the matter good
    As coming solid from the heart ;
Nor would you keep me long in doubt,
    Nor deem my homage overbold,
Though scores of fifty-five, *not out*,
    Leave many a woman proud and cold.

But, Alice, what an hour was that,
　My hour of ventilated vows,
When, beaten thrice, I lost a hat,
　And won a really splendid spouse !
So sing that other which relates
　How, half in pity, half in pride,
You undertook, with choice of dates,
　To be my own, my blooming bride.

Alice sings : " Love that bowls us at the net."

The gentleman resumes :
　Sweetheart, your hand (excuse my back) !
　　This sport, that made us man and wife,
　Did it not yield some prescient smack,
　　Some symbol of our wedded life ?
　For, dearest, in a moral sense,
　　We keep our old relations still ;
　You always break through my defence,
　　Or send me flying where you will !

RUDYARD AUSTIN.

[An attempt to paraphrase Mr. Kipling's *Absent-minded Beggar* for the use of those who prefer what has been called the "ultra-classical bent" of the Poet Laureate.]

WHEN *Rule Britannia* rings through hut and hall,
And men have sung *God save the Queen* withal;
When has been whet the keen invective's sword
Against Meridian Afric's tyrant lord;
Spare not your largess for his kin who plies
The legionary's task in tan-hued guise!
Vague in his views, a man of errant thought,
His best endeavours oft with frailty fraught;
Yet with a conscience facile to forego
The judgment of or us or yonder foe;
Southward, to clean our 'scutcheon, see him
        wind,
Leaving his loved impediments behind!

Scion of Atheling or of menial drone,
Claimant perchance to England's Darling's
        throne—
Five tens of thousands in each other's train
They press athwart the ship-encumbered plain;
With their domestic wants 'tis Alfred's hope
To see your cornucopias cope, cope, cope!

Wives he may have, our Thomas, one or more,
Whose nuptial knot the callous powers ignore;
From which unchartered wedlock—who shall
    say?—
Some offspring may have seen the light of day,
Who needs the warmth Prometheus first con-
    veyed,
With solvent hearth, and Ceres' homely aid.
Doubtless are left some damosels with whom
He held high converse in the devious gloom!
Wrong? was it wrong? I only know they grieve
To miss the pressure of his ambient sleeve,
Who to our care with careless trust assigned
The loved impediments he left behind.

Heir to an Ealdorman or kitchen-thrall—
These crust-distinctions shall we now recall?
What boots it though he left his licensed sire
'Twixt Wapping barmaids serving Bacchic fire?
With claims of wife or wench 'tis Alfred's hope
To see your cornucopias cope, cope, cope!

Myriad the matrons who, in utmost need,
Are nerved by pride to nor complain nor plead!
Their dear Penates rather would they doom
To lie as pledges with a local Oom.
Their brave breadwinner absent, serves but ill
The nation's pittance, practically *nil!*
Vague in his views, a man of errant thought,
He waited not in corners to be sought,

When summoned, much like sturdy Cincin-
    natus,
To leave across his toil a crude hiatus !
Nor lagged to haggle as to who should mind
The loved impediments he left behind.

Life-work of feudal lord or simple serf,
Toilers that race upon, or mow, the turf;
Ceasing their several labours forth they range
From ecurie and mart and moated grange !
Come, with their kindred's wants 'tis Alfred's
    hope
To see your cornucopias cope, cope, cope !

So shall we face him with reproachless hands
(If anything this meaneth) when he lands.
And as returned our Roman, having whacked
The Aequian foe, to find his plough intact,
Likewise should Thomas, Victor, view with pride
His former pair of shoes unoccupied !
Vague, as I said,—a man of errant thought,
And apt, when hurt, to say, *'Tis naught! 'tis
    naught !*
Yet, by our " flag, inflexible as Fate,"
Shall it be said that we have relegate
To pauper's rations, we, his kith and kind,
Those loved impediments he left behind?

Mansion of Crœsus, pastry-monger's cot,
Villa of Earl, in all a vacant spot !

Five tens of thousands in each other's train
They move athwart the ship-encumbered main !
Lo ! with the wants of these, their country's
　　hope,
I bid your cornucopias cope, cope, cope !

STUDIES OF BLIGHTED LIVES.

I.—THE PENALTY OF ACHIEVEMENT.

" To travel hopefully is a better thing than to arrive."
R. L. Stevenson in *Virginibus puerisque*.

I MET Adolphus after many days,
　Him of the roving eye and rippling hair,
Past master in the lore of Woman's ways,
　　　Dapper and debonair.

I think I never saw a man so changed,
　His eye was dull, his locks were limp behind ;
I felt that something must have disarranged
　　　His ample ease of mind.

I grasped him firmly by the flabby hand.
　" Adolphé ! " (in the vocative) I cried,
" What hurt is here that leaves you thus un-
　manned ?
　　　What is the pain inside?

" Has your digestive system been betrayed ?
　Or did appendicitis cause the smart ?
Or have you inadvertently mislaid
　　　Your so prehensile heart ? "

c

Adolphus answered: "Have you never known
   That feeling, when fruition crowns the quest
That just the speculation, this alone,
         Had lent to life its zest?

"Till then existence, full of quiet fun,
   Teemed with potential chances on the wing;
Round any corner you might always run
         Against the Ideal Thing.

"At last the lovely Apparition came.
   Awhile you triumphed; then you woke and
     found
Errantry doomed, and each new day the same
         Drear apathetic round.

"My wife" (I flinched: so sudden fell the news)
   "Is very perfect; yet, if now no more
The Great Adventure's mine, to win or lose,
         This constitutes a bore.

"Time was when, any moment, I might meet
   The woman fore-ordained for me to wed;
That stimulating thought is now effete,
         That *raison d'être* is dead.

"The doctors find my blood has lost its fire;
   They urge a change of air to save my life.
I know my symptoms better; *I require*
         A frequent change of wife."

II.—THE NEW RENAISSANCE.

I SAW him in his yearning youth,
 Before the change that brought the heart's
  ache,
A plunger down the wells of Truth,
 And sworn to follow Art for Art's sake.
O frost that nips the nascent rose !
 O bloom that prematurely blithers !
How could we then forecast the close
 Of Andrea del Resarto Smithers ?

A front like Phidias (ancient Greek),
 A mouth the very mate of Titian's,
A Watteau's chin, a Whistler's cheek,
 A Chantrey's eye for exhibitions ;
Half poet, with the second sight
 Which constantly occurs in Shelley—
He was to be the black-and-white
 Equivalent of Botticelli !

The Editor of *Brush and Plume*,
 A man of sound commercial fibre,
Thought Andrea's art might be a boom
 And catch the better-class subscriber ;
But often, owing to the stress
 Of more immediate local matters,
That graphic print would go to press
 Without his prancing nymphs and satyrs.

Then came the sudden Kodak phase,
    When Art was shelved for Actualities,
The Living-Types-of-Beauty craze,
    Stage Frights and semi-nude banalities ;
Back flew the latest masterpiece
    Enclosed with editorial strictures :
" These contributions now must cease ;
    No further use for fancy pictures."

" The blow, although no blood was spilt,
    Could hardly fail to wring the withers
Of one so delicately built
    As Andrea del Resarto Smithers ;
He bowed before the crushing fates,
    Then rose again by nice gradations,
And now he does the fashion plates
    Published in *Woman's Transformations.*

'Tis true he owns a sumptuous flat
    Who once conversed with gods in garrets ;
I grant he's growing sleek and fat
    On turtle soup and vintage clarets ;
But none the less, when I recall
    The former hopes on which he fasted,
I recognise the moral fall,
    The great career untimely blasted.

III.—THE POLITICIAN WHO STRAINED HIMSELF WITH TRYING TO MAKE UP HIS MIND.

WATERLOO NELSON BINKS, M.P.,
Was as sound a man as you wish to see;
Sprung of a fine old Tory stock,
He held to his father's faith *en bloc ;*
He voted early and long and late,
And whenever he voted he voted straight.

Patriot down to his finger-tips,
He talked of our money and men and ships;
Ascribed the comments of alien Powers
To natural envy of gifts like ours;
And honestly strove to meet the claims
That went with his notable Christian names.

This was the creed of him all along,
That a Tory leader can do no wrong;
Never, not once, was he known to go
Against the Government's *Ay* or *No ;*
Never, in times of darkest doubt,
Questioned what it was all about.

He deemed our skeleton Army corps
A model for European wars;
He counted the Education Act
A miracle due to Tory tact;
And if anyone ventured to say, " You err,"
He called him a Little Englander!

Such was the useful *rôle* he played,
Armed with convictions ready-made;
Never mentally overwrought
By the vicious habit of abstract thought;
Until the moment when Arthur B.
Started his fiscal policy.

But it wasn't so much the hard dry facts
Tempered to taste in rival tracts;
The horrible crux that caused the strain
Which finally softened his so-called brain
Was—How is a stalwart sheep to vote
When the shepherds are grappling, tooth to
    throat?

Till then he had followed his Joe like fate,
But the Duke was also a man of weight;
Arthur was full of the happiest notions,
But who could ignore a name like Goschen's?
He liked his Hicks and he liked his Beach,
But he couldn't see how to vote for each.

Daily a different tub was pounded,
Making confusion worse confounded,
Till in the end his mind gave way;
And I mention, in proof of his swift decay,
That people have seen him, poor old Binks,
Holing out on the Hanwell links!

IV.—A LOST FAITH.

[*The Westminster Gazette*, ridiculing the confidence of
Mr. Chamberlain's supporters in the ultimate triumph of
their far-off purpose, said : "It is sufficient for practical
politicians to consider the next Election."]

As when within the Theban shrine,
  Dim-lit and redolent of spices,
The devotee depressed his spine
  Under the mobile orbs of Isis ;

Till, on a sudden, as his heart
  Into an ecstasy was sinking,
He saw, through some defect of art,
  A priest inside who did the winking ;

Then rose in wrath, and homeward came,
  A disillusionised Egyptian,
And from a cult, so lost to shame,
  Withdrew his annual subscription ;—

So have I known a man or two,
  Who worshipped once with warmth and *brio*,
Then noticed, on a nearer view,
  The mortal *machina in Deo*,

A hollow god of stone or clay,
  Worked like a common showman's puppet—
And so forsook the heavenly way,
  And talked no more of climbing up it.

Such was the case with Ernest Dopes.
  His faith—not any doubt could dim it—
Was fixed on England's soaring hopes,
  To which he traced no sort of limit.

For him the present's fleeting gain
  Was not the end-, nor yet the be-, all;
He passed it by with proud disdain,
  And scanned the Ultimate Ideal.

Ignoring partisan intrigues
  As serving self and not the nation,
The Liberal and the Free Food Leagues
  Alone enjoyed his approbation.

And, since the doctrines there diffused
  Seemed most profound, sublime, eternal.
Nightly, for scripture, he perused
  The page of Mr. Spender's journal.

Judge then of what our Ernest thought
  On reading (roughly) this reflection :
" *Practical statesmen never ought*
  To look beyond the next Election."

Picture the lofty soul that spurned
  Those selfish, sordid aims that suit your
Low politicians, just concerned
  About the mere immediate future :—

Picture his state, how far removed
  From feelings he was used to foster
Before his favourite god was proved
  A hollow earthenware impostor;

Picture—but why disturb the wraith
  Of creeds that death has now encrusted ?
Enough to note a shattered faith,
  A heart irrevocably busted.

A WAGNER DIALOGUE.

[The metrical portion of the following scene is modelled upon Mr. Alfred Forman's popular perversion of *The Nibelung's Ring*, composed, as he puts it, "in the alliterative verse of the original."]

CHARACTERS.

The DUCHESS (*who subscribes to the Opera but never goes near the " Ring "*).

REGINALD (*who is suffering from Rhine-water-on-the-brain, being wedded to an unflinching votary of* Wagner).

THOMAS (*a Footman*).

SCENE—*The Duchess's Drawing-room in Mayfair.*

TIME—3·15 *on a fine Götterdämmerung afternoon.*

The Duchess *is seated in the act of digesting a heavy luncheon. Enter* Reginald, *very haggard from compulsory assistance at the Cycle.*

The Duchess. But, my dear Reggie, how pale you look! And what *are* you doing in evening dress at this time of day? Didn't you get to bed at all last night?

Reginald.   Worn am I out!
      Of afternoon watches
      This makes the third!
      Too soon for the season,
      Ere sinketh the sun,
      Falls at four precisely
      The dusk of the deities.
      Mightless to match
      The will of my wife,
      Hie I to the Hoop,
      To the Waning of Walhall!

Duch.   Reggie, you are wandering.   You are not yourself.   Won't you ring for some brandy-and-soda?

Reg. (*ringing for* Footman).
      Thanks.   Of my throat
      The drought am I fain
      To drench with a nip
      Of the Nothung, or Needful.
        Enter Thomas.

Duch.   Thomas, some brandy-and-soda, quick.
                 [*Exit* Thomas.

Reg.   Numbed by this brew,
      Unshattered my nerves
      Shall be by the shock,
      When the virtueless villain
      Smites in the small
      Of his back the bigamous
      Bridegroom of *Brünnhild*.

Duch.   "*Broonhilda!*"   Isn't she somebody

in Wagner? Of course. I understand now.
Poor dear boy! How you must have suffered!

Reg.　　Ware as a wink
　　　　Of the Wanderer's Wall-eye,
　　　　Discovers my state
　　　　Thy keen understanding;
　　　　The gist of my rede
　　　　Aright hast thou judged.

Enter Thomas: *he pours out brandy, then adds soda
　　till arrested by* Reginald.

　　　　Held be thy hand!
　　　　With measureless waste
　　　　Of mineral waters
　　　　Mar not the mead.

Thomas *retires with an air of not noticing anything
　　unusual.* Reginald *drinks, and at the same
　　time addresses the* Duchess.

　　　　So drain I the draught
　　　　With of slumber the seed
　　　　Sluicing my soul,
　　　　As soused was the wit
　　　　Of *Siegfried* in wassail,
　　　　Enough for my needs
　　　　Till the dolorous dark
　　　　Is spent, and a space
　　　　Of leisureless freedom
　　　　Allowed for refreshments.

Duch.　Poor dear! I agree with every word
you say, though of course I could not have

expressed it so happily. I'm sure I appreciate really *good* music as much as anybody; but I can't stand sitting all that time with the lights down so that you can't see what the women are wearing in the other boxes! No wonder so many of the best people keep away. And then scrambling your dinner just anywhere and any-how! And the daylight so bad for the com-plexion, like the old-fashioned drawing-rooms in the Victorian Era! I must say I *do* think your wife is brave to go through it all. I suppose she gets enthusiastic and forgets every-thing, like people do when they catch religious mania. But you must get dreadfully bored and that, having to pretend all the time. Couldn't you find somebody else to look after her?

Reg.   Like Wotan, but vainly,
   Valorous heroes
   To stick in my Wall-stall
   Hunted I up!
   Answered me each one:
   " This Cycle thou talk'st of—
   Say, is it tuny
   Like to the *Toreador?*
   Or bristles it bravely
   With bountiful ballets?"

   " Honestly," owned I,
   " Tuny it is not;
   Nor yet aggressively
   Doth it, I grant ye,

With ballets abound.
For such name I not
The respectable Norns,
Spinsters at sport
With the skein of their skipping-rope :
Likewise the waterproof
Three little Rhine-maids,
Loosely that watch
Over the oof
With kickless legs
Elusively skirted,
Hardly come under
The heading ye hint of."

So for ward of my wife
A substitute to win
Successless I sought.

But lo! leave thee I must ;
Warns me my watch
That due is the Dusk.
Well I wot for no wight,
Not even for Royalty,
Bideth of ruthless
Richter the bâton.
And loth were I reaching
Late to the Ring
In the whelming night
Mistaking my stall
Unaware to elbow
A wife not my own.

Duch. (*carried away by alliterative sympathy*).
  Tell shall I Thomas
  A cab you to call?
Reg. For a Walkur to whistle
  Need is there none.
   [*He goes out; his voice is subsequently
    heard behind the scenes.*
  Hoyotoho!   Hoyotoho!
  Hi!   Hansom!   Heiaha!
  To the Hall of the Hoop!
  To the Waning of Walhall!
  Hahei!   Hoop-la!   Heiaho!

DIEU ET MON DROIT.

" Say not the struggle naught availeth,
   The labour and the wounds are vain."

[A member of an African firm, in direct communication
with the front, advises his partner during the siege of
Kimberley.]

MODDER camp's by Modder river
   (Brother, brother, sell De Beers !) ;
There the days go idly by,
Hope is sick and like to die—
Brother, should not you and I
   Do a deal and bear De Beers ?

Northward stretch the ghastly levels
   (Brother, brother, sell De Beers !)
Where at dawn our fate was sealed,
Whence at dusk our bravest reeled—
Still the heart-wound might be healed
   If we went and beared De Beers !

Tier on tier the trenches front them
   (Brother, brother, sell De Beers !) ;
There our gallant soldiers sleep,

Yet the price we paid was cheap,
There's a harvest yet to reap
    If we only bear De Beers.

Ill the wind that blows no vantage
    (Brother, brother, sell De Beers!);
Riper yet shall grow the grain
Watered by this ruddy rain,
Ours shall be the future gain,
    Ours who boldly bear De Beers.

Nearer yet the cordon closes
    (Brother, brother, sell De Beers!);
Famine, fever, flame and all—
Graves below the leaguered wall—
Kimberley is bound to fall,
    So are diamonds! bear De Beers!

Later.

Useful news to hand this morning
    (Brother, brother, *buy* De Beers!);
French is working round the right
Fast and keen for a running fight,
They'll be in to-morrow night—
    Now's our chance to bull De Beers!

Take the turning tide of Fortune
    (Brother, brother, buy De Beers!);
Ebbing, flowing—either way—
Some of us should make it pay
Snapping profits while we may—
    Quick, my brother, bull De Beers!

Shall the sole reward be honour?
    Never, never! Buy De Beers!
Rhodes will soon be dealing salmon
Round the hungry haunts of Mammon,
Take my tip—it isn't gammon—
God for England!   Bull De Beers!

LOVE'S LABOUR OF THE FILE.

TIME was, before the Age of Tin,
　Ere Woman took to Bridge or Euchre,
When it was deemed a deadly sin
　To sully Love with thoughts of Lucre;
When cheeks retained the blushful hue
　Which one associates with peaches,
And Eros, open as the blue,
　Had never heard of legal breaches.

The god, as now, was gravel-blind,
　And moved in most uneven courses;
Men changed the thing they called their mind,
　They loved and rode away on horses;
But in those times, which I will term
　The Lion-browsing-with-the-Lamb Age,
Our women scorned to play the worm
　That turns and makes a claim for damage.

When men like Theseus, growing tired,
　Deftly marooned their tearful ladies,
These wed elsewhere or just expired,
　Looking for better luck in Hades;
When Paris went (the heartless brute),
　And scuttled like a common coney,
We do not hear of any suit
　Brought by the derelict Œnone.

Not yet the compromising pen
   Confirmed advances, lightly spoken,
Which could not rise against you when
   Your faith was subsequently broken ;
The living voice conveyed your sense,
   And, if it came to strained relations,
There was no written evidence
   To prove your amorous protestations.

Or if the maiden's heart was hot
   To have her lover's pledge recorded
In less elusive ways than what
   The tablets of her soul afforded—
Or if the gallant felt a call
   To advertise his plighted tryst, he
Chalked up the facts along the wall,
   Or nicked on larches " Τῇ καλλίστῃ."

Turning to later days we find
   That in the course of Love's excursions
Such charmers as were left behind
   Made nothing by these base desertions ;
Thus, when the soldier went on trek,
   Having betrayed the miller's daughter,
Apparently no sort of cheque
   Reached her address at Allan Water.

Gone are the good old rules, and now
   The times (in Walkley's phrase) *mutantur ;*
Our girls in every lover's vow
   Detect the possible Levanter ;

Each careless fragment you indite,
  The simplest ode, the merest sonnet—
They keep it tight in black and white,
  And clap a business-label on it.

The tuft of hair you ill could spare,
  Designed to grace your lady's locket,
The hints of wealth that she should share—
  Each has its pigeon-hole or docket;
And when you wrote in fearless style,
  " Dear heart, my love is strong.   Just try
    me ! "
She stuck your statement on a file !
  O Tempora !   O Labor Limæ !

THE RESTAURANT DE LUXE.

WHEN pessimists your soul appal,
    And England, in a rude decline,
Threatens to stake her little all
    Upon the desperate Zollverein—

O should you ever want to know
    If still the pulse of Empire beats,
Come where the countless shekels flow,
    Come where the flower of London eats !

What man of nicely-balanced wit
    Would deem a nation wholly dead
That night by night consents to sit
    And feed at four pound odd a head—

Not just to titillate the throat,
    Not to evolve superfluous fat,
But to invite the world to note
    That they can pay as much as that ?

Sons of a simple strenuous race,
    Their fancy takes no airy flights,
In all the crowd there's not a brace
    Of conscientious sybarites.

To most the *menu's* terms are Greek ;
    Their orders run—" Bring on your best ! "
They press a button, so to speak ;
    A *chef*, from Paris, does the rest.

Still wines within whose perfume sleeps
  The hoarded South—they pass them by ;
They like the fizzy sort that leaps
  (Bubbles and price) to catch the eye.

Château Larose's ruddy bloom
  May melt the cognoscente's lip,
But has it, right across the room,
  An air of eighteenpence a sip ?

That is the test.   Your actual fare
  Is but a means towards an end,
Which is to prove you do not care
  One paltry fiver what you spend.

Such is our manhood, such the type
  That made and keeps us what we are ;
Who, then, shall say the hour is ripe
  For propping up a fallen star ?

Fair Trade may serve some trivial need
  Such as an Old Age Pension Fund,
But while we boast so brave a breed
  We can't be very moribund.

And yet I feel that fiscal Joe,
  By making trade a touch less free,
Might raise the standard, far too low,
  Of restaurant society.

Why should the perfect millionaire
  Brush feet upon the self-same mats
Or breathe at meals a common air
  With struggling demi-plutocrats ?

Whatever Joseph's aims effect,
    They should achieve this much of good—
To make our Carltons more select
    By putting up the price of food!

THE LITERARY PARASITE.

HE lives within the public eye
   Immune from all investigation
Of how he came to occupy
   That eligible habitation ;
I hear of no accomplished feat
   From which he takes the rank of writer,
Yet almost everywhere you meet
   The name of Mr. Bertram Blighter.

His novel, '*Neath a Woman's Spell,*
   His book of poems, *Past Repealing,*
Those *jeux d'esprit, Half-hours in Hell,*
   That trifle, *Round my Study Ceiling*—
All these are in a harmless vein
   And leave suburban bosoms lighter,
But cannot possibly explain
   The splendid vogue of Bertram Blighter.

No merely adventitious aid
   Helped him to hit the social target ;
His early life is lost in shade—
   I think he went to school at Margate ;
Cambridge has housed him at the " Bull,"
   And Oxford only at the " Mitre,"
And so the praise is due in full
   To just himself—to Bertram Blighter.

How does he do it? I respond—
  " By sitting down with men of letters,
' Author,' ' Omarian,' ' Vagabond,'
  He gets confounded with his betters;
A member of the great O. P.,
  A fixed and resolute first-nighter,
In all accounts of such you see:
  ' We noticed Mr. Bertram Blighter.' "

At what he calls his " five o'clocks "
  You may assist where genii jostle—
The newest Rage in Paradox,
  The final form of Art Apostle;
His knowledge of his guests is slight
  And theirs of him is something slighter,
Yet virtue in a steady flight
  Streams from them all on Bertram Blighter.

A moon amid refulgent orbs,
  A bee among a bed of roses,
Their light and sweetness he absorbs
  And as his own elsewhere imposes;
So, swarming up the rungs of fame
  With ever surer grasp and tighter,
He bears his undisputed claim
  To be " the well-known Bertram Blighter."

THE PIPER OF POSEN,

AND THE PEOPLE WHO WOULDN'T DANCE TO HIM.

AIR (vaguely): *Hamelin Town's in Brunswick.*

I.

POSEN town's in Posen,
And that's a province of Prussia ;
And round this way, as you should know,
A matter of ninety years ago,
The Great Man brought his travelling show
Prior to leaving it badly frozen
Out on the ruthless plains of Russia.
Forts and bastioned towers determine
The range of the city every side,
And through it rolls the Warthe's tide
Washing the place, yet not so well
But the delicate Teuton sense can tell
The taint that comes when the winds are low,
From Slavs and such like vermin.

II.

Poles !
They breed so fast by swarms and shoals,
  And can't be kept in their proper station,

But want a voice—poor ignorant drolls—
   In the working of popular education !
Pay, it's true, their taxes and tolls,
But won't remain like primitive moles
In suitable subterranean holes,
Nor adopt a decently servile air
To German officials planted there
With full permission to ply their staves
On the knuckles of contumacious knaves ;
Forget, in fact, their Helot *rôles*,
      And claim to preach
      Freedom of speech
And the general use of their private souls !

III.

So it happened that one fine dusty day,
   When matters had grown a shade too warm,
William the War-Lord rode that way
   In a terrible Prussian uniform.
And first he called for his mailéd fist,
And gave his moustaches an upward twist,
And cried, as he buckled his burnished glaive,
" I'll teach My Poseners how to behave !
Let not a Slav attempt to show
   (If he wants, that is, to remain alive) a
Nose or an eye as past I go
   Full-rigged, but otherwise like Godiva ! "
And then he rehearsed a speech, " What ho !
Hark ! ye serfs, to the tramp of My retinue,
And the fear of Me and of God I'll beget in you ! "

IV.

On second thoughts he smoothed his brow,
    And sheathed his fist in a velvet glove,
And stuck in his helm an olive bough,
    And said, " I will stoop to win their love!
I'll have My people to make them merry
And greet my pageantry, passing through,
From all available points of view."
And straight he summoned a fleet equerry,
And " Spur," cried he, " to yonder town,
And bid My army and brave police
Not to commit a breach of the peace
Nor shoot, nor maim, nor trample down
More of My Poles than necessary."

V.

And so with suave salute, he
    Led in his league of troops,
And German throats grew fluty
    With *Hochs* and loyal whoops;
But scarce an alien seemed aware
Of the Kaiser's condescending air;
Nothing impressed the passive Poles,
Not even his charger's caracoles;
Never a hip or a haunch went swaying,
So to speak, to the piper's playing;
And though they behaved with perfect tact
Only a sprinkling grasped the fact
That a War-Lord riding there in state
Was a lovable object to contemplate!

VI.

And then in a well-prepared oration
(Other than such as go with the wassail—
Pilsener, not your British crass ale),
Poured in the ear of the Burgomaster,
Whose gratified heart went faster and faster,
He made a regal proclamation,
Allowing the city by special grace
To be no longer a fencéd place—
A scheme that I chance to know was not
Thrown off extempore, on the spot,
While the generous blood ran red and hot,
But one that his wisdom had long ago meant
To put in force when he found the moment
Psychologic and melodramatic
For making the favour more emphatic.
And when he touched on the extra space
And ventured to hope it would meet the case
Of the housing problem, and quickly cure
The ills of Posen's deserving poor—
Why, then on the actual men, it seems,
For love of whom he had launched these schemes
At Heaven knows how much fiscal cost,
This strangely liberal move was lost,
And the thing was a most amazing frost.

VII.

You can take a Pole, as I understand,
And play on his nerves with a German band,
But you can't convert his natural temper or
Get him to jig for a German Emperor.

BEATUS ILLE;

Or, the Truth about Rural Felicity.

Farewell, the City's roar! Farewell,
  Belgravia's meretricious charms!
I come to taste the soothing spell
  That emanates from dairy-farms.

I fling to any summer wind
  The cares that warp my worldly breast,
And look with certitude to find
  That cure of nature—balmy rest.

My palate craves no piquant spice,
  No arts that enervate the town;
What need of Clicquot off the ice
  To wash the native cockerel down?

Fulfilled with milk (a generous tap)
  I seek my chaste and timely bed,
And on the pillow's rustic nap
  Depose a well-contented head.

I leave my little casement wide,
  To catch, athwart the whispering trees
Some murmur of the countryside,
  Somnos quod invitet leves.

Out of my beauty sleep I start !
  Was that the whirr of seraph wings ?
I prick my ears ; I hold my heart ;
  The room is full of flying things !

Bluebottles wanton on the pane ;
  Across my temple flits a bat ;
Along my nose an organ-strain
  Booms from a desultory gnat.

Here, with his head the night-moth bowls ;
  There, I remark the beetle's hum ;
An earwig tentatively strolls
  Outside my sacred tympanum.

I grope for matches fro and to ;
  Three times I bark my brittle shin ;
I draw the blind (of Prussian blue)
  And let the awful moonshine in.

For hours in that religious light,
  One man against a myriad brutes,
I urge the long unequal fight
  Now with my bolster, now my boots.

The moon is down ; my quickened ear,
  Aided by instinct, guides the charge ;
The stars grow pale ; the dawn is near ;
  The bat alone is left at large.

3.25.—The thing has fled
  To seek a more secluded bower ;
Fainting I fall beneath my bed,
  And there remain for half-an-hour.

I wake; I mop my beady brows.
  Is it a " presence " chills my blood ?
Only a brace of neighbouring cows
  Chewing the coarse nocturnal cud.

Under the sheet I veil my head,
  And ask myself why I was born ?
And lo! a blast to wake the dead!
  It is the chanticleer of morn.

Not once or twice ; not vaguely heard
  Performing on a distant hill ;
Four hundred times this shameless bird
  Yells just below my window-sill !

At 5.0 the early ducklings quack ;
  At 6.0 a donkey seems in pain ;
At 7.0 I rise and swiftly pack ;
  At 8.0 I catch the London train.

Welcome, the City's restful roar !
  Welcome, Belgravia's urban charms !
This prodigal shall roam no more
  A prey to Nature's night-alarms !

THE SCHOOLMASTER ABROAD.

[The Steam-Yacht *Argonaut* was chartered from Messrs. Perowne and Lunn by a body of Public School Masters for the purposes of an educative visit to the Levant.]

O "ISLES" (as Byron said) "of Greece!"
   For which the firm of Homer sang,
Especially that little piece
   Interpreted by Mr. Lang;
Where the unblushing Sappho wrote
The hymns we hardly like to quote;—

I cannot share his grave regret
   Who found your fame had been and gone;
There seems to be a future yet
   For Tenedos and Marathon;
Fresh glory gilds their deathless sun,
And this is due to Dr. Lunn!

What though your harpers twang no more?
   What though your various lyres are dumb?
See where by Cirrha's sacred shore,
   Bold Argonauts, the Ushers come!
All bring their maps and some their wives,
And at the vision Greece revives!

E

The Delphic oracles are off,
    But still the site is always there;
The fumes that made the Pythian cough
    Still permeate the conscious air;
Parnassus, of the arduous "grade,"
May still be climbed with local aid.

Lunching upon the self-same rock
    Whence Xerxes viewed the wine-red frith,
They realise with vivid shock
    The teachings of "the smaller Smith";
With bated breath they murmur—"This
Is actually Salamis!"

They visit where Penelope
    Nightly unwove the work of day,
Staving her suitors off till he,
    Ulysses, let the long-bow play,
And on his brave grass-widow's breast
Forgot Calypso and the rest.

In Crete, where Theseus first embraced
    His Ariadne, they explore
(Just now authentically traced)
    The footprints of the Minotaur;
And follow, to the maze's source,
The thread of some profound discourse.

That isle where Leto, sick with fright,
    So scandalised her mortal kin,

Where young Apollo, lord of light,
   Commenced his progress as a twin—
Fair Delos they shall get to know,
And Paros, where the marbles grow.

Not theirs the course of crude delight
   On which the common tourist wends ;
From faith they move, by way of sight,
   To knowledge meant for noble ends ;
'Twill be among their purest joys
To work it off upon the boys.

One hears the travelled teacher call
   Upon the Upper Fifth to note
(Touching the Spartan counter-wall)
   How great the lore of Mr. Grote ;
And tell them, " His are just the views
I formed myself—at Syracuse ! "

When Jones is at a loss to show
   Where certain islands ought to be,
How well to whack him hard and low
   And say, " The pain is worse for me,
To whom the Cyclades are quite
Familiar, like the Isle of Wight."

And then the lecture after prep. !
   The Magic Lantern's lurid slide !
The speaker pictured on the step
   Of some old shrine, with no inside ;
Or groping on his reverent knees
For Eleusinian mysteries !

Hellas defunct ?   O say not so,
　　While Public School-boys faint to hear
The tales of antique love or woe,
　　Brought home and rendered strangely clear
With instantaneous Kodak-shots
Secured by Ushers on the spots !

LIPTON UNLIMITED.

Pride of Britannia's element (the Ocean),
  At what incredible expense and pains,
Sir, you have roused to maritime emotion
    The Viking in our veins !

Mixed nature, like the versatile Phœnician,
  Blending with trade the instincts of a tar,
You keep intact that mercantile tradition
    Which made us what we are !

Reared on a fundamental base of tea-leaves,
  Your tower of fortune scales the arduous sky,
Till on the Hook off which your copper keel
    heaves
    Two Worlds have fixed their Eye.

Not since the heirs of freedom fairly shivered,
  Waiting on Trafalgar's supreme sea-test,
Has England's universal marrow quivered
    With such a strange unrest.

With flaming cheeks or else unearthly pallor,
  Our youth, recalling Nelson's brilliant fight,
Couples that Viscount's mention with the valour
    Of Thomas Lipton, Knight.*

* Subsequently Bart.

I have known public men of light and leading,
   Accustomed at ephemeral themes to scoff,
Turn absolutely giddy just with reading
      The pregnant phrase—THEY'RE OFF!

People of irreligious mind, whose nerve is
   Such that they never know when they have
      sinned,
Gravely perused the Church of England Service
      To find a prayer for wind.

We loathed the breeze too light to lift a feather,
   Longed for the spanking kind which you
      prefer,
And asked why what is known as *Shamrock*
      weather
      Seemed never to occur!

Upsprang at last a twenty-knotted blizzard,—
   Lee-rails awash beneath the scudding brine;
And hope pervaded every patriot's gizzard,
      Warming his blood like wine.

Fathers, unused to these nocturnal capers,
   Up perilous suburban chimneys clomb
To see your efforts told by halfpenny papers
      On the recording bomb.

Infants, neglecting early bed and bottle
   To play their part in this historic scene,
Would watch the preconcerted signals mottle
      Old Thames with red and green.

Sharp envy overtook the moon at rising :
   A myriad counter-fires usurped the view ;
So many took this chance of advertising
     Their wares as well as you.

From height to answering height the signs went
    streaming,
   From " Hampstead's swarthy moor " to Wre-
   kin's pile,
Till " the red glare on Skiddaw " set blaspheming
    " The burghers of Carlisle."

Bear up ! Sir T. ; remember Bruce's spider ;
   Build further *Shamrocks* through the coming
   years ;
Virtue like yours, though long retirement hide
   her,
     Ends in the House of Peers

THE DEMORALISATION OF ROBERT.

[Lines suggested by Lord Onslow's remonstrance to his fellow-magistrates on the subject of the attitude adopted by the police towards motorists in the wilds of Surrey. Among other things he contended that "the effect upon the police of constantly acting as spies must be demoralising." The following verses are affectionately inscribed to Colonel Lewin, of the Surrey Bench.]

Bill Sykes addresses the Earl of Onslow :—

MELUD, yer got 'em on the 'op !
    Yer Surrey mites is much to blime,
Lettin' the self-respectin' cop
    Go slippin' into pawths o' shime.

Mind yer, I'm not agin the beaks,
    They goes as strite as they ken see ;
They ain't no bloomin' set o' freaks,
    But mostly 'uman, sime as me.

My tistes is simple like a bibe's,
    I pads the 'ighway, 'eel an' toe,
I loathes yer scorcher's noisy gibes,
    I scorns yer giddy lokermo.

But when I'm on a thinkin' job
    An' wants ter sniff a bit o' breeze
I 'ites ter see a copper's nob
    Bobbin' abaht be'ind the trees.

It 'urts my feelin's as a bloke
  What loves the peaceful country wys,
When Niture's charms is mide a cloak
  Ter screen a hambush packed with spies.

What's wuss—an' 'ere I blime the beak—
  I sees a simple artless rice
Put on ter ply the shidy sneak
  And lose their hinnercence an' grice.

Yer never knows where things 'll stop
  When once yer tikes ter low deceit;
Yer starts in life a honest cop,
  An' ends with rubbers on yer feet.

Yer gits ter 'ave a crawfty heye
  Prahlin' at nights rahnd harear-stairs,
Shiftin' yer slops from dy ter dy
  Ter nick a hartist hunawares.

Melud, I sees it clear as glawss;
  So, if yer wants ter use my nime,
Tike it, and sive a decent clawss
  From slippin' dahn the pawths o' shime.

LOCKS ON THE IMAGINATION.

[A Birmingham barber, who counted Mr. Chamberlain and Mr. Jesse Collings among his *clientèle* and possessed samples of their hair in his collection of personal relics, was the victim of a violent assault by highwaymen, in the course of which he was robbed of a bag containing the implements of his profession.]

LET other gifted misers,
    Attached to purple thrones,
Secure the busts of Kaisers,
    Or Kingly chicken-bones ;
For them I feel no jealous gall,
    No trace of bile I bear,
Who have upon my parlour wall
    A slice of Joseph's hair.

The Thing is sleek and raven,
    Yet unbedewed with dye,
And o'er it, fairly graven,
    His image, eye to eye ;
And, from the pen whose lightest whim
    Can make the world to rock,
My letters-patent, signed by him
    Who grew the actual lock.

Hard by, a bunch of tresses,
    Culled from a kindred soul,
Recalls the crop of Jesse's
    Superbly ashen poll ;

And in a missive, very rare,
   This epoch-making mem. :—
" *You are to come and cut my hair*
   Next Friday, 10 a.m."

I sport no fiscal favour,
   Follow no chieftain's charge ;
My business is to shave or
   To shear the race at large ;
Concerned with outward form, as such,
   I pouch impartial fees,
And yet it needs a statesman's touch
   To handle heads like these.

Dear relics !　Round you lingers
   A not unnatural pride !
How near my scissored fingers
   Came to your scalps' inside !—
The brain that broached the Tariff schemes,
   The thoughts that swelled the brow
Which　harboured　once　that　dream　of
   dreams,
   Three acres and a cow.

And you, ye rude garotters,
   Knights of a lawless quest,
Who jumped with craven trotters
   Full on my fallen chest ;
I grudge you not your paltry swag ;
   Ye dealt me grievous knocks,
Ye racked my bones, ye reaved my bag,
   Ye dared not rape those locks !

TO CHRISTINE.

[An Offering from her Bachelor Uncle, who, in default of the power to immortalise her through the intrinsic merits of his verse, consoled himself by enshrining her in the deathless pages of Mr. Punch's Almanack.]

CHILD of the silk-soft golden hair,
　　The sweet grave face, the hazel eyes,
Mother of dolls, a constant care
　　That makes you prematurely wise;

(Although your brother, younger yet,
　　Adopts an independent tone,
And begs you will not always set
　　Your wisdom up against his own)—

I take delight to touch with you
　　On divers themes, and well I may;
It is your charming habit to
　　Believe exactly what I say.

When you enquire with thoughtful brow
　　What any given object is,
Why it was made, and when, and how,
　　And other cognate mysteries;

When by your manner you imply
　　That nothing known to mortal men,
Or even seraphs up the sky,
　　Eludes my penetrating ken;

Forgotten hopes renew their bloom;
   I feel I have not wholly failed;
"There still is one," I say, "from whom
   My awful ignorance is veiled.

"As yet no disillusion saps
   A faith pathetically stout,
And several seasons must elapse
   Before she gets to find me out."

So from our converse I abstract
   A sentiment akin to joy,
Fleeting, I own, and, as a fact,
   Not unencumbered with alloy.

For memory probes an ancient sore
   Connected with my distant youth;
I, too, should like to be once more
   A quiet searcher after truth;

Once more to learn in various schools
   The things rejected by-and-by
When I discovered certain rules
   Which the exceptions stultify;

Found Nature with herself at strife
   (To take a single case) and woke
To the depressing view that life
   Must be regarded as a joke.

A blight possessed my eager soul;
   My fancies took a fatal twist;
And I assumed the chronic *rôle*
   Of what is called a humorist.

For you such fears are far away;
    Your faith and your digestion thrive;
But then I'm forty, if a day,
    And you, of course, are only five.

Still, here's the best I can in rhyme;
    And when (how rare the angels' calls!)
You come again at Christmas-time
    To greet the dear familiar walls,

You'll take my verse for what's it's worth,
    And, though you find it barely sane,
You'll raise a decent show of mirth
    To spare the author needless pain;

And lift your tiny silver mug,
    Graven with mine, the giver's, name,
And toast my health, and bid me hug
    The patient hope of coming fame;

And I shall answer, " Dear, you see,
    My future lies behind my back;
But here's *your* immortality
    In Mr. Punch's Almanack!"

1901.

COVERT LOVE.

HERE, where the woodland's flanking lines
  Have left a little space of blue,
Between the shadows of the pines
  With beating pulse I watch for you;
With beating pulse, yet unafraid,
I wait you in the silent glade.

I shall not hear your footstep fall
  Upon the matted mossy ways;
A stir of branches, that is all,
  A flutter through the threaded maze;
My heart will know that you are near;
Be sure I shall not miss you, dear.

What sound is that of severed leaves
  Across the depths of sylvan dark?
Is it a dream that fancy weaves,
  Or do her angel pinions—Hark!
I hear the sudden warning ring,
" *Hen forward!* "   D—, I've missed the thing!

WIGS ON THE DOWN.

[Written in honour of an "emergency camp" of the
Inns of Court ("Devil's Own") on Perham Down,
illustrating the supreme advantage of education and
individual intelligence in a private soldier, as freely
demonstrated in the Transvaal War. The system, which is
the subject of these lines, has since been greatly modified.]

"Soldier, soldier, from Salisbury Plain,
    Seared with the battle's feigned alarms,
How have they taxed your legal brain?
    What have you learned of the lore of arms?"

" I have learned to clean utensils, I can rinse a
    stewing-pan,
    I can black my fighting boots and scrub a
    floor,
I can wash a sickly haddock like a self-respecting
    man,
    I have mastered (in a word) the art of War."

"Barrister, barrister, come from the camp,
    Man of intelligence, gently bred,
Trained in the school of the midnight lamp,
    How have you learned to use your head?"

" I can air my frugal blanket at the crowing of
    the lark,
    I can polish up my basin till it shines,

I can grub for rotting refuse from reveille on to
    dark
  As I scavenge, scavenge, scavenge down the
    lines."

  " Chancery junior, back from the field,
    How have you fared in the well-wrought
      trench ?
  What are your lessons like to yield
    Brought to a test by the raiding French ? "

" I can lay my kit in detail in an Army-pattern row,
  I can put it out and pack it up again ;
Which is always useful knowledge when you
    come to face the foe,
  And it hardly causes any mental strain."

  " Q.C., Q.C., fresh from the fray,
    What of the last strategic views ?
  What do you know of the war-game's way,
    Feint and cover and counter-ruse ? "

" I can shoot at restful objects (when the sergeant
    gives the range),
  I can recognise a front attack at sight,
I can even look for cover, though you mustn't
    make a change
  In your regulation distance from the right ! "

  " Gentlemen Templars, gallants all,
    Stout-heart Lincolns, and English Grays,
  Eager to serve at your country's call,
    What have you learned these fourteen days ? "

F

" We have learned to slice a rasher, we have
    played the (Oxford) scout,
  We have plied the menial muck-rake with the
    best,
We have lost superfluous tissue (we are nothing
    like so stout)
  And our brains have had a pure and perfect
    rest ! "

OUR LAST LINE OF DEFENCE,
IF NOT DEFIANCE.

[Being the Views of a Private of the Inns of Court.]

" LIGHTS out!" rang our bugles ; the weather
    was drizzly,
  And deep lay the dark round the Devil his
    Own,
As we flung ourselves down on our bedding at
    Bisley—
  The sleepy to slumber, the wakeful to groan.

I could hear the low curse of the Common Law
    sentry,
  Our shield from the peril that prowleth by
    night,
As I dozed with my section of militant gentry
  In skirmishing order, undressed by the right.

With a smile on my conscience—the outcome of
    duty—
  And blisters that burned at the back of my
    heel,
I evoked recollections of laughter and beauty
  In scenes where I once had a succulent meal.

F 2

And I thought of the dear ones that urged me to
    spare a
  Brief respite of leisure from legal routine
For a cursory trip to the blue Riviera
  Or Fontainebleau's woods at the first of the
    green.

Had I carelessly yielded to feminine clamour
  And placed before England's my personal
    gain,
I could now have been basking in Italy's glamour
  Or haunting the splendid Alhambra (in Spain).

But my ear had been closed to the voice of the
    charmer,
  My breast was as basalt, my will like a rock;
I would up with my rifle and on with my armour
  And out on the warpath at six of the clock.

For I thought, "What if France, at the Easter
    vacation,
  With Ministers loafing in various lands,
Should arrive overnight, and from Cannon Street
    Station
  Ask London at breakfast to hold up her hands?

" But, if only they hear that our corps is in fettle
  Scarce thirty miles off from their line of retreat,
They will certainly shrink from essaying the
    mettle
  Of us who have never acknowledged defeat.

" Yet 'tis we that Officials regard as a burden,
  A raw, ineffective, civilian police;
They would stint us and starve us, forgetting the
      guerdon
  Rome gave to her loyal, if amateur, geese."

*   *   *   *

So I dreamed till the blast of the blatant reveille;
  Then rose from my pallet, one uniform ache,
And repaired to parade with a vacuous beille
  For England and home and my honour at
      stake.

DUCI REDUCI.

To Lord Kitchener of Khartum.

Air—*Une Marquise* (Austin Dobson).

I.

Homeward bound from overseas,
          K. of K. !
Lightly let the sequent breeze
          Round you play ;
You who know what danger is, K.,
  Yet have never learned to swoon,
May the bounding deeps of Biscay
  Find your martial maw immune !
Do not dash anticipation—
          So they pray
Who have sketched your debarkation
          Ere the day ;
Who with eagle nerve have nicked you
  By a fine prophetic swoop,
And (for Friday next) depict you
  Sternly gazing from the poop.
Come before our joy is jaded,
          K. of K.,
And the flush of Peace has faded
          Into gray !

Shall the poet's faith be stamped on
   Who accosts your urgent keel?
Will you stultify Southampton,
   Where the Mayor has booked a meal?
Where in terms profuse and brainy
   He prepares to greet you thus:
"Scipio South-Africané!
   Welcome! you are one of Us!
Take our freedom: we adore you!"
               He will say;
All of which is bound to bore you,
               K. of K.

Yet, because we want you home,
Do not dally with the foam;
Let delay no longer test us,
Rise like Venus in her cestus
              "'Crost the Bay."

II.

You're a worker from of old,
               K. of K.
Pomps and pæans leave you cold,
               K. of K.
You would like to land in mufti,
   You would hurry down the dock
Not in trappings, plumed and tufty,
   But in checks and billycock!
And you haven't, now It's over,
             Come to stay;

Nor to lie at length in clover,
But to change your train for Dover,
                        K. of K.
For, although the work's appalling
    Which should have you here at hand,
Yet you've heard the East a-calling
    Out of India's coral strand ;
And, as soon as time and place
    Let our feelings find release,
And we've called you, to your face,
    First in War and First in Peace,—
Thither where the Empire needs you,
                        K. of K.,
And your own " *Ubique* " * leads you,
                        Lies your way !

* Alternative motto of the Engineers.

THE HARBOUR BAR.

REFLECTIONS OF A PATRIOT ON THE DOVER REFRESHMENT BUFFET.

" BREATHES there the man with soul so dead,"
　　So lost to purely English graces,
Who does not, when he deigns to tread
　　Among the tracks of foreign races,
Thank Heaven nightly on his knees
That he is not as one of these ?

Too great to count them food for mirth,
　　Mere stuff to whet his Attic wit on
(Since none may pre-arrange his birth,
　　Or be, by taking thought, a Briton),
Our patriot's heart, from pride exempt,
Feels pity rather than contempt.

Brought up on British beef and fog,
　　He shudders through his very vitals
At *fricassées* (presumed of frog)
　　And "made-up" plates with fancy titles ;
" What hope," he asks, " for men who take
No true delight in chop or steak ? "

He roams their galleries of Art,
　　Calls them so French, so free in morals,

Misses the themes that move the heart,
　　Kittens at Play, or *Lovers' Quarrels*,
The healthy air, well worth the fee,
That breathes from *our* Academy.

He samples literary plays
　　And finds the English version vicious,
Roundly condemns the Rostand craze
　　And deems D'Annunzio meretricious;
He hankers for a homely scene
Bristling with "Soldiers of the Queen."

But most his heart within him burns
　　When at the last, a home-sick rover,
Back to his country he returns
　　And stands upon the pier at Dover,
Watching what vision first will stir
The envy of the foreigner!

With large proprietary airs
　　He sees the Frenchman, pale as flannel,
Who shunned the Calais-Buffet's snares,
　　And fasted all across the Channel,
Now swoon with joy—his haven won—
At sight of Dover's Tea and Bun!

"THE EQUAL RIGHTS OF MAN."

[In the following lines an attempt is made to reproduce
the unreasoning but unshakable attitude of the rustic maid
in Wordsworth's *We are Seven*.]

An artless, dull, mechanic fool,
   By Union catchwords caught—
Why should he want a better school
   Of economic thought?

It was a gracious morn of Spring;
   The hour was half-past six;
Some men were on a scaffolding
   Engaged in laying bricks.

My fancies, soaring with the lark,
   Recurred to common soil;
I felt I could not but remark
   The dignity of Toil.

Anon I set this thought aside,
   Observing one that cast
Reproaches on his mate and cried,
   "'Ere, stow it! not so fast!"

"Good friend," I said, in wonder lost,
   "I am concerned to know
What is the cause why you accost
   Yon earnest workman so.

" If to be idle were a sin,
    I naturally ask
Why you should want to check him in
    The middle of his task ? "

" Guv'nor," he said, " you take my word,
    It's time 'e 'ad a rest ;
It ain't no manners in a bird
    To queer his neighbour's nest.

" If 'e don't mend 'e 'll 'ave to quit ;
    I know 'is nawsty tricks ;
'E works too rapid ; 'e's a bit
    Too 'andy with 'is bricks !

" Take it from me, that's why I'm put
    To check 'is little plan,
An' stop 'im tramplin' under foot
    THE EQUAL RIGHTS o' MAN ! "

" If in the act of laying bricks
    He tastes a human joy,
Would you propose," I said, " to fix
    A term to that employ ? "

" Read what the Union bosses say ! "
    That simple swain replied ;
" They lets us lay so much a day,
    And not a brick beside.

" 'E'd like to knock the stiffuns out
    By layin' all he can ;
I tell him straight, ' 'Ere, 'ow about
    THE EQUAL RIGHTS o' MAN ? ' "

" Your case," I cried, " betrays a flaw
    The souls of men are free;
You seem to overlook the law
    Of manhood's liberty.

" On Competition's eager head
    You place a tyrant's ban."
" That's 'ow our motto runs," he said—
    " ' THE EQUAL RIGHTS o' MAN !' "

" But you ignore," I answer made,
    " You place upon the shelf
The promise of celestial aid
    To him that helps himself.

" Each should improve what hours he may
    Within his mortal span."
Vain words ! he still would have his way :
" That's what the Union bosses say—
    ' THE EQUAL RIGHTS o' MAN !' "

THE LAST OF THE DURBAR LINERS.

[Dedicated, with affectionate compliments, to the author of *The Sailing of the Long-Ships*.]

THEY heard the sirens singing, they saw the barges rock ;
Society (a remnant) stood weeping by the dock ;
Away, away, to silence melted the City's roar,
And blasts of briny ozone came whiffling round the Nore.

" I come from various quarters that reek of English fame "
(This was the Blizzard speaking ; he knew the sites by name) ;
" I noticed all the landmarks, just where they used to be
When your remote forefathers arranged to rule the Sea.

" They sailed with Cœur de Lion, they ran the old Crusades ;
They shipped with Admiral Hawkins on sundry sporting raids ;

They served with Drake of Devon (Devon for
    wind and rain !)
And helped themselves unhindered to half the
    spoils of Spain.

" They raked Gibraltar's ridges, they shot and
    burned and rammed ;
They roused the Nile from slumber long ere the
    thing was dammed ;
Long ere ye got your highway where Joseph's
    bark has gone,
They had confirmed the Charter secured by
    honest ' John.'

" Fair-minded were your fathers, great gentlemen
    at play,
They never growled in mangers, 'twas not the
    Sea-dogs' way ;
But, while they grudged no foeman the stuff they
    counted trash,
They fought like fiends for credit, they worked
    like wolves for cash.

" Heirs of the valiant Sea-Kings (assembled here
    on board),
Lo ! in their wake ye follow, if not with fire and
    sword ;
Armed with the tiffin-basket, the fine mosquito-
    net,
Ye still conduct the Empire whose suns refuse
    to set.

" Your fathers fared in frigates, they went in
    homely guise,
With ' Victory or the Abbey ' ever before their
    eyes ;
To-day with trunks and trousseaux safely insured
    ye go,
Pacing in soft apparel upon a P. and O.

" The Sea-Kings drew their sabres, they dealt
    the frequent dint ;
Ye too would leave impressions wrought in a
    rarer mint ;
The East, so short of colour, shall fall about
    your feet
To catch the Carlton manner, the mode of
    Curzon Street.

" Ye go to see and win her with culture from the
    West,
To lift the load of languor that lies upon her
    chest ;
Hope not too much ! She'll suffer that temporary
    strain,
Then turn (a local habit) to ' plunge in thought
    again.'

" Ye cannot all be Josephs, to do what he would
    do,
To take and make an old world nearly as good
    as new ;

But ye may share the feelings that lately filled
    his head
When longing (under hatches) to join the mighty
    dead.

"So, outward bound or homeward, through
    scenes ye know by name,
Observe the panorama that reeks of English
    fame ;
Do note the ancient landmarks just where they
    used to be
When your sublime forefathers arranged to rule
    the Sea."

G

SHYLOCK AND THE POUND
OF SOUL.

[Reflections on the Education Bill Debates.]

DEAR human child, whose woolly head
  Closely recalls the unweaned lamb ;
You with the lips whose native red
  Is stained with inexpensive jam ;

O virgin soil, O plastic clay
  Within the primary potter's grip,
To whom, for moulding, day by day
  So unsuspectingly you trip ;—

When I remark the limits set
  About your elemental lore,
As that from two and two you get
  A total tantamount to four ;—

When I perceive your nascent nerve
  Engrossed with dates of Britain's Kings,
The pothook's iterated curve,
  And other non-contentious things ;—

I fondly hope you never dream
  That your prospective moral state
Still constitutes the steady theme
  Of loud and bellicose debate.

It lies, I trust, outside your ken
　　That nightly, till the senses reel,
Six hundred heated Christian men
　　Wrestle for your immortal weal.

Yes, when on Heaven's name they call
　　And knock each other's doctrines flat,
You are their object ; it is all
　　On *your* account, unconscious brat !

Summer will pass, and Winter's hand
　　Of dying Autumn take his toll,
And still, like Shylocks, they will stand,
　　Claiming their punctual pound of soul.

I wonder, should you come to know
　　The facts about this deadly feud,
Whether your little heart would go
　　And burst with speechless gratitude ;

Or rather, being made aware
　　What means they used to reach their ends,
You would compose a tiny prayer
　　To be delivered from your friends ;

And crave permission of the star
　　That on your recent advent smiled
Just to continue what you are—
　　A simple, bounding, heathen child.

A NOCTURNE AT DANIELI'S.

[Suggested by Browning's *A Toccata of Galuppi's.*]

CARO mio, *Pulcinello*, kindly hear my wail of woe
Lifted from a noble structure—late Palazzo
    Dandolo.

This is Venice, you will gather, which is full of
    precious " stones,"
Tintorettos, picture-postcards, and remains of
    Doges' bones.

Not of these am I complaining ; they are mostly
    seen by day,
And they only try your patience in an inoffensive
    way.

But at night, when over Lido rises Dian (that's
    the moon),
And the vicious *vaporetti* cease to vex the still
    lagoon ;

When the final *trovatore*, singing something old
    and cheap,
Hurls his *tremolo crescendo* full against my beauty
    sleep ;

When I hear the Riva's loungers in debate
    beneath my bower
Summing up (about 1.30) certain questions of
    the hour ;

Then across my nervous system falls the shrill
    mosquito's boom,
And it's "O, to be in England," where the may
    is on the bloom.

I admit the power of Music to inflate the savage
    breast—
There are songs devoid of language which are
    quite among the best—
But the present orchestration, with its poignant
    oboe part,
Is, in my obscure opinion, barely fit to rank as
    Art.

Will it solace me to-morrow, being bit in either
    eye,
To be told that this is nothing to the season in
    July?

Shall I go for help to Ruskin?   Would it ease
    my pimply brow
If I found the doges suffered much as I am
    suffering now?

If identical probosces pinked the lovers who
    were bored
By the sentimental tinkling of Galuppi's clavi-
    chord?

That's from Browning (Robert Browning)—I
    have left his works at home,
And the poem I allude to isn't in the Tauchnitz
    tome;

But, if memory serves me rightly, he was very
    much concerned
At the thought that in the sequel Venice reaped
    what Venice earned.

Was he thinking of mosquitos? Did he mean
    their poisoned crop?
Was it through ammonia tincture that " the
    kissing had to stop "?

As for later loves—for Venice never quite mislaid
    her spell—
Madame Sand and dear De Musset occupied my
    own hotel!

On the very floor below me, I have heard the
    patron say,
They were put in No. 13 (No. 36, to-day).

But they parted—" *elle et lui* " did—and it now
    occurs to me
That mosquitos came between them in this
    " kingdom by the sea."

Poor dead lovers, and such brains, too! What
    am I that I should swear
When the creatures munch my forehead, taking
    more than I spare?

Should I live to meet the morning, should the
    climate readjust
Any reparable fragments left upon my outer
    crust,

Why, at least I still am extant, and a dog that
    sees the sun
Has the pull of Danieli's den of " lions," dead
    and done.
Courage ! I will keep my vigil on the balcony
    till day
Like a knight in full pyjamas who would rather
    run away.
Courage ! let me ope the casement, let the
    shutters be withdrawn ;
Let scirocco, breathing on me, check a tendency
    to yawn ;
There's the sea ! and—*Ecco l'alba!* Ha ! (in
    other words) the Dawn !

TO A PIGEON OF "LA PIAZZA."

BIRD of the beady eye and tireless crop,
Capacious past the common pigeon's use ;
Brave, neck and breast, with bloom of green and
    purple,
A rounded Iris answering the sun,
But suited for the rest in sober grey,
Mating the dusky gleam of Moorish domes,
And sombre-hued against the gilt and glare
Of bastard Byzantine, restored " to taste "—
I like you, bird ; the gondolas and you
Would seem the only ancient things in Venice
Which we may hope to understand without
The help of Mr. Ruskin. Let me buy
One little paper bag of yellow maize,
Dear at a *soldo*, and I'll undertake,
Waiving the Master's aid, to win your love
As perfectly as though I had by heart
The Inwardness of all the Middle Ages.

I say, I like you, bird ; you have a soul
Unseared by culture ; you will roost o' nights
Indifferently on a marble niche
Flanking the dim mosaic's awful marge,
Or up a rain-spout ; on the Doges' Palace,
Or Quadri's restaurant ; you throw your eye

With equal and dispassionate regard
Upon the untutored Briton who aspires
Not far beyond the sudden Kodak's film,
And on the fair Bostonian rapt with awe,
Her *Stones of Venice* tucked beneath her arm,
Her visage wan with having drunk too well
The borrowed sweets of that laborious bee,
Augustus J. C. Hare.   It moves you not,
Although La Duse passes, deadly bored
With playing in her hero's *Città Morta;*
Nay, should the hero's self, Italia's pride,
D'Annunzio, most superb and rather bald,
Consent to prance across the dazzled square,
Recalling memories of the Golden Time,
You would not turn to stare as others turn,
Quite rudely; what's D'Annunzio, pray, to you,
Unless his largess leaves you plump with grain?
And even so the studied attitude
Will certainly escape you.   I respect
Your disregard of persons.   I admire
With what aloofness you ignore the crowd,
Going about your private loves and hates
As though the public counted not at all,
Save as a menace to your fragile toes
And as a source of food.   It is an art,
This unselfconsciousness, which we have lost,
Like that of wearing wings. You keep them both.

What brought you here, I wonder, at the first,
Before the hucksters spread their toothsome
    wares

Within the very temple's outer courts?
Doubtless the prose accounts are always best;
Yet, were I poet, I would dare to say
Here, too, was instinct, Nature's work by which
Beauty is drawn to beauty, like to like,
Not knowing wherefore.   So, by such a spell,
I will believe that in the Time-old tale
Those Cytherean doves, they knew not why,
Hovered about the gracious ways of her,
That other Aphrodite of the Sea.

TO MR. PUNCH ;

EXPLAINING HIS PERPETUAL YOUTH.

[Lines written for a performance given under Mr.
Punch's auspices at the Palace Theatre on behalf of the
Hospital for Sick Children, Great Ormond Street,
May 3rd, 1900.]

PRINCE of the board that groans with fatted
    calf,
  Nicked with the knives of Thackeray and
    Keene,
Where, waxing stout, we constitute the Staff
  On which your lusty limbs affect to lean,
                    O Evergreen—

What potion drawn from what immortal pump,
  What roseate pill, what draught of ruby wine
Works in your veins that thus your hallowed
    hump
  Of senile dotage gives no sort of sign
                 At fifty-nine ?

I know a secret culled from Nature's book,
  Whereby the hunted creature, timely wise,
By way of self-defence assumes the look
  Of those respective spots in which he lies,
             Or feeds, or flies.

The rabbit grubbing in the grizzled copse,
  On gaudy boughs the garish cockatoo,
The weasel like the earth from which he pops,
  The khakied warrior on the dun karoo—
                    Of such are you !

For you, whose chosen haunt is childhood's
      heart
  (Witness to-day, and this memorial scene),
Playing in children's guise your veteran part,
  Amid the bolts of Time you move serene,
                    Dear Evergreen.

SWEETNESS AND STRENGTH.

[Among the more clamorous topics of the holiday season
must be reckoned the important questions, " Should
Women Work ? " and " Should Kissing be Abolished ? "
The inter-relation of these two problems has not yet been
adequately recognised.]

GONE is the giant gooseberry's girth,
    And gone the brave sea-serpent's gambols ;
Themes that command a rarer mirth
    Pursue us on our summer rambles ;
To-day we drink new problems in
    With apprehensions nicely polished,
And ask *Should Women toil and spin ?*
    Or else, *Should Kissing be abolished ?*

Myself, untaught in chemic terms,
    I shrink, from lack of education,
To probe the peril, due to germs,
    That lies in casual osculation ;
With equal reason I refuse
    To treat of economic questions—
But when it comes to *moral* views,
    I teem with luminous suggestions.

Go back in thought to Eden's bowers,
    And with Mosaic history grapple ;—

You'll find no talk of working-hours
  Till after Eve had plucked the apple ;
For so the tale, that tells us how
  Her form she first began to drape, runs ;
And surely kisses sealed her vow
  Before she took to stitching aprons.

O yes, we learned it long ago,
  (Prior, indeed, to Girton College),
How half our sweets and bitters flow
  From tampering with the Tree of Know-
    ledge ;
The need to work, the right to kiss—
  We've caught them from our common
    mother,
That as the penalty for this,
  And one the medicine of the other.

Divorce the two, and take from toil
  Its only satisfying guerdon ;
Or filch from love its proper foil—
  And life, each way, becomes a burden.
Excess in either art alone
  (Consult the Lunacy Commission)
Greatly impairs the mental tone,
  And ultimately means perdition.

To illustrate the perfect type :—
  Her kiss should be as soft as vellum,
While thirsty readers pluck the ripe
  Fruit of her busy cerebellum.

O supple lips ! O seething brain !
   Yet if, perforce—no laughing matter—
I had to choose between the twain,
   I'd cheerfully resign the la ter.

THE CHANTEY OF THE NATIONS.

A CORONATION SONG, 1902.

GREAT BRITAIN.

SONS of the Blood, which is twice as thick as
    water is,
Lock, stock and barrel of the Race that rules the
    Sea !
    Ye have left your occupation
    At the Mother's invitation,
Left the ice-floe, and the swamp, and the jungly
    mango-tree !

I am the Bard, it is I that make the Catalogues,
I that give the Oracles that otherwise were
    dumb ;
    I am Kipling, I'm the Voice,
    I'm the Chosen People's Choice,
I'm the Words and Music also, I'm the Drummer
    and the Drum.

What I have said I have said, and pretty often
    too,
Hinting of the heritage that goes with British
    birth ;
    But to-night it might be pleasant
    To address the Nations present
Who are not as yet embodied in the Lordliest
    Thing on Earth.

FRANCE.

Thus saith the Voice to the genial Boulevardiers :
" Welcome, gallant neighbours, I've a word to
    say to you :
    Could ye get your gutter Press
    Just to lie a little less,
Ye might soon forget Fashoda, and the shock of
    Waterloo."

AUSTRIA.

Thus saith the Voice to the braves of Francis-
    Joseph Land,
Dwellers by the Danube in the home of cakes
    and bock :
    " Ye have shown us what to waltz to,
    But ye have your little faults too,
And ye sold us Hungary chargers, five-and-forty
    pounds a crock."

H

ITALY.

Thus saith the Voice to the men of V. Em-
    manuel :
" *Ye* are not fair-weather friends, ye stick through
    storm and rain ;
      Ye have lent our land the Duse,
      And we could not well refuse a
Debt of honour, so we sent you our Corelli and
    our Caine."

GERMANY.

Thus saith the Voice to the Teutons of the
    Fatherland :
" Hail ! Kaiser's men, out of Berlin on the Spree ;
      If your students thirst for knowledge
      By a course at Oxford College
They might learn to know us better and behave
    more cousinly."

RUSSIA.

Thus saith the Voice : " Ye have seen us, O ye
    Muscovites,
Seen our Thameski Prospect and the City paved
    with Tin :
      Ye have marked the friendly air
      We adopt towards the Bear,
Will ye veil in turn the Tartar underneath your
    velvet skin ? "

JAPAN.

Thus said the Voice to the wearers of Chrysan-
    themums :
" East is West and West is East, for now the
    twain are one ;
    We are white and ye are yellow,
    Ye are young and we are mellow,
Yet we'll hold the Seas together for the Lion and
    the Sun."

AN IDYLL OF THE CHIEF.

THE JOUSTING AT THE BRIDGE.

So on a day Sir Belchamp Porte-drapeau
Drew with his faithful remnant, what there was,
To that weird battle down by Westminster.
And o'er his head, he going delicately,
The banner of the great C.-Bannermanship
Drooped; and athwart its folds the clan's device,
A sporran'd haggis fluttered, and, below,
The Campbell is a-coming ran the script.
But from his sinister arm was slung the shield
That bore for blazonry a barbéd fence,
And therewithal the rede, *J'y suis, j'y reste.*
And by his side the sword *X-calibre*
(For so they styled it, since in point of proof
The blade was deemed an unknown quantity)
Swung like a pendulum; and on his flank,
As one that should beguile the Chieftain's gloom
With jest and ribald joyaunce, lightly rode
That loyal knight Sir Lab de Boom-le-vrai
In devious caracoles; and as he rode
Now hummed a jocund air—*Peers, idle peers,*
And now with aching midriff laughed aloud
At " forty millions, mostly flannelled fools ";
So swift his fancy played.

But he, the Chief,
Heard, or heard not, and either way was deaf
To jest and ribald joyaunce.   Yet he heard,
Or out of mist-like memory seemed to hear,
Far-off a voice that ever in his ears
Rang hollow from the trenches, crying "Spades!"
And in a muse, low muttering to his heart :
"O me! for much has changed since bold Sir
      Brum
Clave to the Table Round ; and much again
Since I, with those four knights, Sir Cop-la-
      Poule,
Sir Fife, Sir Gris du Jeu-de-Paume, and him,
Sir Durdans, newly named of Chesterfield,
Rode out to break the heathen !   Now I hear
How these, with others, loyal-seeming all,
Are leagued against me, while the heathen wait
To rise and take the breathless victors on.
An evil chance it were for any chief
To move against his own elect and strike ;
For so the hurt he deals he deals himself
Two-fold or even more, which needs must be
Most painful."

Then Sir Lab, that overheard :
"What plaint is this, my Chief, of rival powers?
Light was my lord of Durdans at the best,
And under any name would be as light.
I count him but the foam that flecks the wave,
Dazzling a while, but shortly doomed to pass
Adown the wandering wind.   But you, my liege,

I know you for the dark unfathomed deep
That may not easily pass."

                        Thereat the Chief:
" O ay, not easily pass, not easily pass,
If visions hold.   Methought a moon agone
I jousted at the Bridge with certain churls,
And had, for mate, Sir Durdans; and the score
(Two points to twenty-six and one game up)
Favoured the heathen slightly.   Then I dealt,
And, dealing, drew a hand of five small hearts,
Topped by the ten, and all the residue
Damnably dull, and gazed thereon, and passed.
But he, the dummy, found a voice and cried,
' Spades!' and those others doubled.   So we
       twain,
Who looked on imminent ruin, said, ' Content ! '
Meaning the opposite.   Whereat the foe
Led straightly forth and made a mighty slam,
And filched the rubber, smiling.   Then I sware,
Saying I never more would pass the choice,
To dummies like Sir Durdans.   Nay, Sir Knight,
Henceforth I shall not easily pass, not I."

ODE TO A LIBERAL MOCKING-BIRD.

[On the return of a Tory Government to power for the
second consecutive time. With respectful compliments to
F. C. G. of the *Westminster Gazette*.]

[After Keats.]

OUR brain aches and a torpor numbs our nerve
    As though with opiates we were deep imbrued,
Being apparently condemned to serve
    A second shift of penal servitude;
And we must envy thee thy happier lot,
    Gay-hearted Dryad of the trenchant plume,
      Who still upon the post-meridian breeze
In thy green-tinted plot
    Amid the Opposition's ambient gloom
      Chaffest the Tory with thy usual ease.

O for a drink of water such as cools
    The Liberal larynx torrid on the stump,
Smacking of Cockermouth's perennial pools,
    Of Wilfrid Lawson and the village pump!
O for a tankard full of H_2O,
    The true, the proletarian Hippocrene,
      With Local Veto winking at the brim
And filtered mirth below;
    That haply we might hop about the scene
      With thy sublime agility of limb:

Hop as our heart dictates, and quite ignore
    What thou hast missed this many a summer-
        tide,
The weariness, amounting to a bore,
    Of being always on the stronger side;
Where fat and callous-eyed indifference rusts
    Even the Tory Blood's incisive blade:
       Where humour's bolt is evermore dis-
        charged
At unresisting busts;
    And wit that works by opposition's aid
      Dies of a liver horribly enlarged.

Frankly, immortal Bird, for five long years
    We had a presage we should die that way,
And now the country's voice confirms our fears
    Almost allowing us to fix the day;
Now more than ever longingly we dream
    Of times when Victory flushed the Liberal
        camp,
    And there was ploughing in the sandy ruts;
Of Rosebery, grateful theme,
    Of Harcourt on the vulnerable ramp,
      And all the vista lined with obvious butts.

For thee, a like regret would seem absurd;
    No vast majorities depress thy brain;
Thou hast (if one may say it of a bird)
    Thy faithful subjects in the Powers that
      reign.

Perhaps the self-same art in days by-gone
  Tickled the ribs of Joseph's brother-band,
    When o'er a coat of many patterns blent
His pictured optic shone
  Through comic casements opening on the land
    Of Goshen, where he ran the Government.

The Government! The word is as a knell
  Tolling us back to dulness of the Pit,
While thou art happy in another spell
  Of the old hope forlorn that whets the wit.
There is thy Joseph, hewn a hundred times,
  And, like Valhalla's warriors, fresh as paint!
    Ah! in thy gallant fight against the gods,
Pity our bloodless rhymes,
  That fall on hollow squadrons, pale and faint,
    With never a chance to front the frowning
      odds!

PARADISE AND THE SNAKE.

"Serpent, Sir!" repeated Mr. Pott . . . "I said,
Serpent, Sir—make the most of it."—*The Pickwick Papers*.

[The Preferential Tariff question, so far as Ireland was
concerned, would be considered not on its merits, and not
as a question of "Imperial policy," but the votes and
support of the Irish party would, in the forthcoming
struggle, be given with a sole view to the interests of
Ireland, and more especially to the speedy restoration of
Irish legislative independence.—*Mr. John Redmond.*]

WE drew a Paradise in dreams,
 The home of love and settled law,
Of pearly bogs and peaty streams
 Flooded with milk and usquebaugh;
Where Limericks made a lasting mirth,
 And shamrock-time was never over,
And bulls of thrice the usual girth
 Habitually browsed on clover;—

Where rents were paid with punctual joy
 Accompanied by festal jigs,
And bailiffs lost their late employ,
 And every green was bare of wigs;
Where, as before the primal curse,
 The lambkin loafed beside the lion,
And Wyndham, in a kilt of Erse,
 Embraced a fully-breeched O'Brien.

A Paradise of dreams—no more!
　For at the waking hour we find
The same insidious Worm that wore
　A hole in Adam's peace of mind;
Though Eden renovates her youth
　In yonder green and billow-swept Isle,
There still the Serpent whets a tooth
　Characteristically reptile.

Not Kingly feet that pressed her shore
　Avail to dry that venom up;
Not gifts of Saxon gold galore,
　Not even Mr. Bennett's Cup;
Mid blessings showered on man and brute
　In that uniquely pampered country,
There blooms a sole forbidden fruit,
　And Something coils about that *one* tree.

The old familiar "Taste and see"
　Wheedles the gardener where he delves—
"Sample this brand and you shall be
　Like to the gods that rule themselves!
The other sorts—pear, peach, and nut,
　Reluctant doles of niggard misers,
Are, relatively, nothing but
　Mere pregustative appetisers!"

*　　　*　　　*　　　*

O Isle of Erin, could the star
　That smiled upon your earlier lot

Restore, by way of Avatar,
   St. Patrick, that illustrious Scot !
For snakes he had a drastic bane
   That took, I hear, a deal of beating ;
Ah, might he give them once again
   A course of more than earthly Keating !

WHEN WE SLEEPING BEAUTIES AWAKEN.

[Lines written for a dinner of the Stage Society.   With acknowledgments, for the title, to the Master.]

THERE was a time, as I am told,
  Back in the dim Victorian Age,
When antic Custom, dull and cold,
  Wrapped like a pall the British Stage ;
And some among the best " reporters " said :—
" Dramatic Art is practically dead ! "

But ere they fixed the funeral site
  A race of Thinking Men arose,
Clapped on the corpse a searching light
  And found her simply comatose ;
(Four years ago they took this fearless line,
That is to say, in 1899).

Before the lapse of many days,
  The Sleeping Beauty stirred in bed
And used the Tennysonian phrase :
  " O love, thy kiss would wake the dead ! "
From Mr. Whelen came that Clarion sound ;
His was the smack that brought the lady round.

They fed her up (for she was weak
  And swelled with swallowing windy puffs)

On German, Belgian, French and Greek,
    On Norse and even native stuffs;
With urgent appetite the patient drank in
Essence of Hauptmann, Heijermans and Hankin.

Exotic fish and local fowl,
    With these they plied her generous maw—
Curel and Barker, cheek by jowl,
    And Ibsen jostling Bernard Shaw;
Thus, if *The Lady from the Sea* looked foreign,
For British Matrons there was *Mrs. Warren.*

Her moral frame expanded too
    On transcendental meat and drink;
Of thoughts that ranged quite near the blue
    She caught the missing Maeterlinck;
And after meals of more than earthly manna
Inhaled the stiffish fumes of *Monna Vanna.*

Taught, in *The Good Hope's* crib, to know
    The salient signs of healthy growth,
With every second word or so
    She rapped you out a ribald oath;
Showing that, should her other powers go wrong,
Her language still could " suffer and be strong."

Such is her progress, large and free,
    Whose nerve, of late reduced to pulp,
I now and here propose that we
    Should drink in one exhaustive gulp;
Long may her history, freed from hoary fossils,
Live in the Acts of You, her Young Apostles!

THE PLUTOCRAT AT THE DINNER-TABLE.

[After the manner of Robert Browning's Monologues.]

I.—IN PARK LANE.

AND so your neighbour charmed you? 'Tis
    a type
Instinct with sound commercial qualities,
And dowered with every solid bridal grace
Good to restore the fortunes of a line
Noble in name but out at elbow-joint,
Groggy o' thews, thin marrowed, run to seed
For lack of lusty graft on senile stock,
Yet keeping what of wit sufficed to know
The price of antique curios cornered tight,
Intrinsic worth of crusted quarterings,
And what the legend's tag was like to fetch—
How goes it? "*Foy et loy*"—old Norman style.
And so you found her charming? What! I'm
    wrong?
'Twas not the Countess pleased your sense of
    style,
But just your other neighbour? Why, my
    friend,
That was the governess, called at sudden pinch

From meal i' th' nursery regions, tea and eggs—
To supplement our numbers, thirteen else.
O but of course a lady, need I say?
A thing imperative for the children's sake,
Who ask correction, being apt to lean
Too much for speech and manners on the maids.
Good family—goes back, I understand,
Five hundred years or more—stout yeoman
          stuff;
Had chance of title, but declined the same
On ground of being unversed in brewers' ways;
Nay, more, concealed the offer so refused,
A case of false pride, happily rare enough
In business circles.   Brief, their fortunes fell
(Value o' land depressed, the old excuse)
On indigence, the genteel-piteous kind,
Bringing the eldest daughter down to this,
A post of five-and-forty pound a year
With beer-allowance.   Sweaters' wage, you'll
          say,
And scarce a third of salary paid my cook?
Why, there I'm with you, were I free to waive
What rules, imposed by economic law,
Provide a check for thoughtless altruism,
Which else had rashly pauperised the girl
Or spoilt the market-rates for poorer men.

          But to resume our Countess.   'Tis a type
Instinct, I said, with sound commercial sense,
In whose " combine " with yonder belted Earl

You have a sign o' th' times who runs may read;
Our ancient orders, visibly corrupt—
How says the Laureate?—yielding place to
    new!
Alchemy's trick of good red blood infused
In old nobility's veins; fresh Phœnix-flights
Of fowl revived—the Eastern fable serves—
By breath o' th' spirit o' commerce blown on ash.

    Frankly it is a patriot's part they play,
Our merchant-princes, who restore the breed
By taking noblemen for sons-in-law!
How else re-galvanise the Upper House
Closed, this long while, against commercial
    claims,
Letting what prime financiers prop the state
Go unennobled, save by Nature's work?
Ay, there's the price we placid Tories pay,
And something too serenely through the nose,
For huge majorities, not greatly prone
I' th' naughty pride of members to recall
By just what manner o' process they arrived.
Were I indifferent to my country's weal,
Or less the loyalist you know me for,
Almost I might be moved to shift my flag
Into the camp of men so deep in need,
The battlements they storm so steep to win,
And, being narrowly won, so hard to hold,
They could not well afford to disallow
Its due equivalent to service done!

I

Well, well, one rambles on in idle talk.
The wine is with you.   No?   Then, if you
    please,
We'll join the ladies.   You shall prove me right
Who praised the Countess.   'Tis a type, I said,
Instinct with—— What?   The governess again?
I fear you must excuse her.   She withdraws
Straight from the table to her proper place
On these occasions, by my wife's desire,
Who shrinks to trespass on her leisure time.

II.—WITH THE WORSHIPFUL COMPANY OF PORKMONGERS.

How do you call the book?   *Our Uncrowned
    Kings?*
'Tis new to me, who have but little time
Reserved from higher claims to keep abreast
With novel lines in literary goods.
A satire?   Ah!   I never greatly cared
For humour, notably such as leaves the mind
Vaguely aware of swift allusions lost,
Impalpable airy flights supposed of wit;
Clearly a state obnoxious to repose,
Being apt to cause diversion o' blood to brain,
Needed elsewhere to aid the liver's work
After your dinner, Nature's only hour
For reading.   What?   It's clever stuff, you say,
And levelled at the new plutocracy?

Well, 'tis the penalty we're mulcted in,
We of the wealth that tickles envy's ire,
Harmless, I hope, for whoso has his feet
So firmly planted he can well consent
To pay what silent pity greatness owes
To ignorant detraction found i' th' mouth
Of who, poor devils, after all must live.
Doubtless they have their figure, not too long,
If one but cared enough to buy them out.

Young D'Arcy wrote it? Why, I know the
          man;
Dined with us in the Lane—Lord only knows
Just where the women pick these scribblers up!
Came in and out, a tolerated guest,
Till he forgot his manners, had the face
To please my daughter, and was shown the door.
That's how, being entertained on sufferance,
They glean what little lore they boast to have
Of good society, and go their ways
And shamelessly profane its mysteries
In books like this! I say, you're never safe
If once your footmen let them pass the hall.

Mind, I distinguish. I refer to men
Professed of letters, not the other sort,
Mere social mercenaries I employ
(Paid by the Press in cash, by me in kind—
A dance, a dinner, even a simple crush)
To make a paragraph's advertisement,

Telling an eager public how I dine,
Who—and their jewels' value—graced my board,
Or under what unequalled wealth of flowers
The staircase laboured when my wife received.
With such I make no war; they earn their feed;
And, though they use what tact the case demands,
Impose on none that moves within the pale.
But when I see an open welcome given
To struggling men of literary tricks
In houses commonly presumed select,
Why, there's a snobbery finds me justly wroth,
Who recognise that subtlest form of pride
Which bids remark its status how secure,
How unassailably proof against assault,
Since it allows itself to ope its doors
(No man's opinion asked) to whom it will,
Highway or hedge, made worthy for the nonce
By that approving seal the house confers.
Rank snobbery, so say I !

                              Yet here again
I make a nice distinction, please to note ;
Holding that even writers may be classed
In different ranks according to deserts.
How judge this difference, otherwise obscure,
Save as we millionaires apprize success
By tangible results that take the eye ?
Thus there are authors, as I understand,
So skilled to gauge the reading public's views
And what new turn the market's like to take,
Making supply anticipate demand

Upon a scale so noble, that their art
Assumes proportions almost fit to wear
The higher style and dignity attached
To Commerce proper.   Such a type as this,
Since prejudice is impotent to floor
The unanswerable logic of results,
I'd not refuse to meet, no matter where;
Nor would our Chairman, having thrice my
      wealth,
Yet strangely free from pride for one so great.
Rumour indeed alleges he was born
With literary tastes he might have turned
To lucrative employ, yet chose to be
The amateur and gentleman he is.
You'll see him soon with what fine modesty,
As though oblivious how the nations gape
For awe of private monarchs like himself,
He bids you charge your glass to drink the King!

A RELIC OF THE TERRACE.

I SAT upon the river's bastion'd marge;
  A solemn peace possessed the torpid air,
Save when a few strange oaths from off a barge
        Lifted my hair.

Sweet haven from the Chamber's human hum,
  Here to this spot, with light refreshment
    spread,
The heated legislator loves to come
        And cool his head.

" Breathless with adoration "—ay, to me
  The phrase applied as well as Wordsworth's
    nun—
I watched them on the Terrace, taking tea
        And toasted bun !

Oft had I pictured their heroic make
  Who keep Britannia going on the blue;
And now I *saw* them, eating currant cake,
        Like me and you!

Think, if a mortal brushed against a god
  Under Olympus, how his heart would glow !
But if the gracious presence even trod
        Upon his toe—!

It was a Minister who stood on mine!
    Mere joy, for all my anguish, held me mute;
And now I worship, in a Trilby shrine,
                    That shattered boot.

My burning heart supplies its vestal flame!
    Calverley, when he viewed with venial pride
His Prince's cherry-stones, had much the same
                    Feeling inside!

UPON AUGUSTUS

[Greatly cheered by the invention of a watch as thin as a crown-piece, to take the place of the ordinary sort that spoils the figure].

[After Herrick.]

WHENAS AUGUSTUS deigns to go
In beauty's pomp, sublime and slow,
Along the lists of Rotten Row;

Or, like a flower with dew besprent,
Exudes a steady blast of scent
Down Piccadilly's pavement;

Much I admire that wondrous dress
Whose lambent folds do more express
Than veil the figure's daintiness.

And musing on him, line by line,
I think how many arts combine
T'adorn that human shape divine.

Soothly some woman, over-laced,
Advised him how to have his waist
In yon exiguous zone encased.

Some fair, that had no pouch to hide
Her proper kerchief, armed his pride
'Gainst pockets that do bulge inside;

So as the key is passing small,
The which, emerging from the Mall,
He lifts his nightly latch withal.

Some coins he hath, for chariot-fare,
Deftly disposéd here and there—
The rest is paper, thin as air.

And, since it causeth inward pains
To carry such a watch as strains
That region where the middle wanes,

Now hath he got a little one,
Whereof the bulk doth scarce outrun
A wafer's fine dimensión.

When in his mirror he observes
His form inclined to ampler curves,
Augustus shaketh in the nerves;

And, lest he mar his comely guise,
He summons all his strength, and tries
A little massage exercise.

So doth he labour to reduce
Whatso is like to grow profuse,
And serveth not for beauty's use.

Herein he hath a wide success—
Save for his brains, whereof I guess
No power on earth could make them less!

THE BIG LOAF'S LABOUR LOST.

[On the defeat of a Liberal by a Labour Candidate at Barnard Castle.]

HE laid his ivory pen aside
With the air of a man of easy pride,
And toyed with the ponderous chain of gold
Hid in the waistcoat's ample fold.
The roseate hues of moral health,
That colour, at times, the haunts of wealth
When the heart is light and the conscience clear,
Pervaded the general atmosphere,
And hovered about the haloed Head
Of Skinner & Progmore, Limited.

Starting as messenger, *ætat*. 9,
At a local store in the grocery line,
Fate had fostered his early hope,
Based on pickle, and crowned with soap ;
And now his sovereign hand controls
A couple of hundred score of souls,
At wages that cover their weekly bread
With a bonus for funeral rites when dead.
And at present he calmly awaits the hour
When the People's Party returns to power

With a trifle down on the debit side
For several sinews of war supplied,
In token of which, if they don't forget,
They're bound to make him a Baronet.

And here I should like to give the closing
Words of the speech he was just composing
Against a possible early date :—
" Free and enlightened Electorate !
Myself a son, I may say, of the soil,
My heart goes out to the men that toil !
Burdens enough you have to bear,
But your Bread should be free as the light and
    air !
Shall we be false to the faith of years,
Bought with our fathers' blood and tears ?
Shall we surrender our hard-won gain
For the charlatan bribes of a Chamberlain ?
No ! we will baffle his base intrigue,
Under the flag of the Big Loaf League ;
Firm to the mast that flag is glued ;
Let us fight beneath for the People's Food ! "

He had laid his ivory pen aside
With the air of a man well satisfied ;
And turned to his favourite print to read
His evening portion of fiscal creed,
Happy to know he was like to find
Nothing to shake what he called his mind,
Or lead him to think that the spheres had stirred
Since Cobden uttered the final word ;—

He turned, as I said, to his favourite print,
Graceful in tone and green in tint,
And at once emitted an angry snort
(Humour not being his special *forte*)
As his eye discovered the rather droll
Result of the Barnard Castle Poll.

" This Labour fellow that heads the list "
(So mused the heated philanthropist)
" Comes of a class whom men like me,
Promising loaves that are large and free,
Flatter and pamper and stroke and pet,
And here is the kind of thanks we get.
The Led Dog bites a hole in his Leader !
The Fed Babe goes and swallows his Feeder !
Oh, sharper far than a cobra's fang
Is the graceless conduct of such a gang !
Do they imagine, when all is said,
That the pains we spend on the People's Bread
Are just for their pleasure—to take and use
And drop and be done with when they choose,
With never a care for the sport they spoil ?
To h—l, I say, with your Sons of Toil ! "

Such were the thoughts (I give their gist)
Of the disillusioned philanthropist !

THE ACTOR-MANAGER DISCOURSES.

I.

[The following homily is addressed to an author of
established reputation who has applied his gifts to the
production of an original literary drama not unworthy of
Shakespeare, but betraying ignorance of the modern
requirements of the British stage.]

WE have perused your meritorious play
With that impartial condescension which
Our sense of justice leads us to bestow
On budding talent; but it will not do.
Yet, if your ignorance be well advised
To draw instruction out of present failure,
Our words will not be wasted on the wind.
And, first, to rectify a false conceit
Frequent enough in literary men
Who look on drama as a branch of letters,
Whereas, in point of fact, their lower art
Is but the menial handmaid of the stage—
Were Shakespeare (who is fortunately dead)
Among the living candidates for fame
His plays would not command a button's pur-
    chase.
We patronise him with the deference due
To the immortal Dead who take no fees;

While on the credulous audience he lays
The spell of antique unction like a church
Whereof the priestly management supplies
A splendid ritual, careless of the cost.
Hence the success he still achieves despite
His damnéd gift of literary style;
Also despite his pestilential habit
Of holding mirrors up to human life,
A daring enterprise, as you have proved
Whose work betrays this woful want of tact.

For, please to mark the plays whose facile run
Is as the going of a god on wheels.
Do their inventors draw from actual life?
Sir, they are men of business; they adopt
The safe conventions of the story-books,
The only certain shaft to perforate
A British bosom.
                    Take our soldier-author,
Our *Second in Demand*, if we allow
The leading place to Shakespeare—does he let
His military knowledge mar his play,
And give us soldiers such as they are found
Extant in visible barracks?   No, not he;
He knows his theatre too well for that.
He has his finger on the pulsing heart
Of myriad clients clamorous for the type
Long-hallowed by the shilling novelette,
Crystallised in the monthly magazines
By woman's fancy soaring past the facts!

If we detect in your submitted work
A fault more obviously patent than
Your fatal gift of reproducing Nature,
'Tis the intolerable craving for
Originality.   Your business is
Not to invent ideas, but rather watch
Those vital movements in the tastes of men
Which, followed fast enough, conduct to for-
    tune;
To sniff the presage of them on the breeze,
Tracing a tendency toward Musketeers,
A hankering after good old Drury Nells,
An urgent boom in left-off mistresses
Rudely resurgent on the wedding-eve.
These things are in the universal air
Subtle as patchouli, appealing to
A lot of sentient playwrights all at once.
So, too, the law that regulates the plot,
Confining it to well-established themes,
Applies with equal force to dialogue;
The public likes to recognise a friend,
Not to be made to think.   That was the rock
On which the argosy of Bernard Shaw,
Packed with unminted specie, went and split.

Once more, beware of letting poetry,
Especially the blanker sort of verse,
Disturb the claims of those interpreters
On whom your hopes depend.   Their primal
    task

Is to arrest attention on themselves,
And not divert it to the author's work.
Though exquisitely conscious how a line
Should be enounced, a noble jealousy
Might paralyse them with the fear that you,
Rather than they, should earn the pit's ap-
    plause.
We here allude, of course, to poetry
Designed to penetrate the average brain,
Not to the loftier kind which tends to leave
The public nervous, like a little child
Vaguely aware of tricks imposed upon it.

Further—a common error with the scribe—
Your play reveals a total disregard
Of the peculiar faculties of those
On whom the duty of " creation " falls.
Thus, we have failed to find a leading part
Composed to illustrate *our* special gifts,
And offer scope for that high power of passion
By which it is our undisputed pride
To hold the women's throbbing hearts in
    thrall.
To merit patronage a man must write
A drama *round ourself*, as Greekish art
Upreared a suitably receptive shrine
About the sacred Image dropped from heaven.

In fine, you lean too much to Nature's ways
Who lets no mortal dominate her stage

But loves to deal her entrances and exits,
And much between, without respect of per-
    sons.
Art, on the contrary, discriminates,
Lifting the Actor-Manager aloof
From those inferior persons in his pay
Who have no just occasion to exist
Save as the negligeable satellites
On whom his scintillating talents play
(Since even genius demands a foil);
Who herald his approach, and in his presence
Veil their identities, and stand aside
For culminating curtains all his own.
Thus are the facts of life improved upon,
Art's noblest function being to correct
An oversight of Nature. Try again.

II.

MADAM, you must not count me cold of heart
Nor deaf to beauty's homage frankly paid,
If with an equal frankness I decline
That proffer of the soul's surrendered pride
Which shows you gifted with a fine contempt
For maiden modesty. It cannot be.
Yet I am mortal (in a way) and wear
No certain armour, any more than you,
Against the stab of beauty, save alone
My solemn sense of service owed to Art.

K

But were I once to give my pity play,
Once to allow my ruthless front to melt,
I dare not think what issues might evolve
From such a precedent.

                 Believe me, Madam,
Your case is not by any means unique.
Unnumbered missives, much the same as yours,
Breathing insidious scents of Araby,
Perfume my dressing-room.   The nightly door,
Whence I debouch on my attendant brougham
Reveals a wistful ambush on the watch,
To see the Artist, so to speak, unveiled,
Human and palpable as other men,
Yet more disquietingly beautiful ;
To stand a moment in the mystic flame
That is my envelope, and there imbibe
The benison of air that I have breathed.

  Nay, if I told you of the provinces,
What I have suffered where my advent is
Like heavenly visits, relatively rare,
And time admits no devious processes
But by his fringe   must   needs   be   rudely
    gripped—
It would surprise you.   I have been pursued
By swift admirers, not to be denied,
Right into my hotel, and stood at bay,
A hunted thing, until the telephone
Summoned the brave police and they arrived,
And drew a compass round my chaste retreat.

I mention this to salve your stricken pride
By solace drawn from numbers ; you will see
That, as I said, your case is not unique.
For me, though not precisely celibate,
I still must hold myself in high reserve.
I live for Art : my soul is not my own
To give at pleasure ; it is consecrate
To nobler uses.   That, again, is why
I never boast about those private charms
Of person and deportment which provoke
Feminine flattery, but seem to me
To win their only worth from being placed
At Art's disposal unreservedly,
With all emoluments attached thereto.
Sworn servitor of One, and One alone,
At Her tremendous feet I lay my gifts,
Content to be the minister who takes
Vicariously the homage meant for Her ;
To be the happy medium by which
As through a filter, drained of vulgar dross,
The general worship percolates Her way.

An illustration.   There was once a temple
Sacred to Phœbus.   It contained a priest,
Himself a fair Apollo, lusty-limbed,
And, like the god's own laurels, evergreen ;
A constant source of desperate concern
To fluttered ladies in the holy haunts.
Think you he took the lightest cognisance
Of carnal adoration ?   Not at all.

K 2

His eyes were on the altar, unaware ;
Or, if he guessed what passions he inspired,
He feigned a child-like innocence, and said
" Apollo's be the praise ! " and passed it on.
So I, who humbly tend the shrine of Art,
Not curious how my earthly charms may work
Havoc in heads susceptible as yours—
I give the glory where the thing is due,
And serve my ministry, and have my soul
Single in Her employ Whose priest I am.

A *PUNCH* STAFF-COLLEGE.

[At University College School, whose Head Master at
the time was Mr. Lewis Paton, formerly Captain of
Shrewsbury, a prize was given for a series of cartoons,
the Masters being admissible as models. It was won by
a son of Mr. A. S. Boyd, whose work is familiar in the
pages of *Punch*.]

PATON, your hand! I never thought
    That in our midst we had a School
Where adolescence might be taught
    So charmingly to play the fool!

Not since, by far Trinacria's shore,
    Great Dionysius held the throne,
Has Art enjoyed such license, or
    So suave a " tyrant " set the tone.

Your hand, I say! and here's my heart
    (Warm with the afterglow of lunch)
That yearns to hymn your glorious part
    As patron of a School for *Punch*.

In one dear scene our lots were cast,
    Where Severn nursed her old renown,
And still the unforgotten past
    Outwears the pedagogic gown.

Else how should you so well disarm
    The schoolboy at his wanton game,
And take from sin its secret charm
    By stamping it with virtue's name ?

But here is genius ! here a touch
    Of what the gods alone bestow ;
For, while Salopia taught you much,
    She never taught you this, I know.

Nay, if my memory plays me true,
    The scheme to which your tastes are wed
Directly stultifies the view
    Held by our venerated Head.

For, had our young Hellenic sen se
    On fancy-portraits been employed,
We should have earned a recompense
    Other than that of Master Boyd.

Discovered, from his awful seat,
    Limning the Chief in furtive wise,
Whatever promise marked the feat,
    Ten " penals " would have been our prize !

Forgive me, if I call from sleep
    Indecorous thoughts of days long done ;
You have your dignity to keep,
    While I have, obviously, none.

Yet though, in life's estranging maze,
    At sterner tasks you toil and spin,
Our common love of laughter's ways
    Leads me to hope you count me kin !

And if in " letters more humane "
   You've passed my little range of skill
I like to think your ampler brain
   Approves an art humaner still.

Macte ! and ever may the round
   Of graver duties leave you free
So to support a training-ground
   Of younger Tenniels yet to be.

TO AUSTIN DOBSON.

After Himself.

[Rondeau of Villon.]

At sixty years, when April's face
   Retrieves, as now, the winter's cold,
   Where tales of other Springs are told
You keep your courtly pride of place.

Within the circle's charméd space
   You rest unchallenged, as of old,
         At sixty years.

Not Time nor Silence sets its trace
   On golden lyre and voice of gold ;
   Our Poets' Poet, still you hold
The laurels got by no man's grace—
         At sixty years.

1900.

LINES IN MEMORIAM

QUEEN VICTORIA.

BORN 1819.   DIED JANUARY 22, 1901.

THE tears we disallow to lesser ill
  Here is no shame for English eyes to shed,
Because the noblest heart of all is still—
    Because the Queen lies dead.

Grief asks for words, yet silent grief were well;
  Vain is desire, as passionate prayer was vain;
Not all our love can bring, by any spell,
    Breath to those lips again.

Ah! had but Death foregone his royal claim,
  Demanding ransom, life for life the price,
How loyalty had leaped to kiss the flame
    Of such a sacrifice!

God knows, in many a need this thing has been—
  Light hearts for her have dared the desolate
    grave;
From other hurt their blood has saved the Queen;
    From Death it could not save.

And of the dregs to drink from sorrow's cup
    This is most bitter, that with life's release
She might not leave her children folded up
            Between the wings of Peace.

Yet, for a solace in that darkest hour,
    When even Kings have found themselves
    alone,
Over a people's love she kept her power
            Firm as her fathers' throne.

So by the gate where is no first nor last
    And lords of earth must lay their splendour
    down,
    Thither, where Love is Sovereign, she has
    passed
            To win his queenlier crown.

Thence, by her guardian spirit, heavenly-wise,
    Still shall her realm of old be girded round,
And common loss yet closer knit the ties
            That common love has bound.

Yea, too, since Nature owns no bar of race,
    She, being dead, may speak through alien
    lands,
Changing suspicion, by remembered grace,
            To trust that understands.

O great of heart! in whom the world has known
    Wisdom with woman's sweetness reconciled;
Who held her Kingdom's honour, as her own,
            Still fair and undefiled!

Best shall they keep that stainless memory
    bright
  Who count their heritage a holy debt,
Who walk with fearless soul the way of light
        In which her feet were set.

And in that faith, ere yet our tears are dry,
  Or poignant grief has spent its sudden sting,
To Him she serves we lift our hearts and cry,
        " God save her son, the King ! "

JOHN RUSKIN.

Born 1819.   Died January 20, 1900.

Amid the stress of high-embattled strife
　　Thy gentle spirit finds its long release ;
So ends the quiet labour of a life
　　　　That loved the things of Peace.

Her triumphs were thy own ; the bloodless fight
　　For Truth and Beauty thou hast waged and
　　　　won ;
Careless of praise ; content before the night
　　　　To know thy task well done.

Nature to thee was holy ground, and Art
　　An act of worship wrought within the shrine ;
To thee, if given to God with perfect heart,
　　　　Such service shewed divine.

Those temple-rites, not meet to be profaned,
　　Still hast thou taught with sacerdotal pride ;
Still fed the fire, still kept the robe unstained,
　　　　And by the altar died !

SIR ARTHUR SULLIVAN.

BORN 1842.   DIED NOVEMBER 22, 1900.

In the immortal music rolled from earth
  He was content to claim a lowly part,
Yet leaves us purer by the grace and mirth,
  Human, that cling about the common heart.

Now on the bound of Music's native sphere,
  Whereof he faintly caught some earthward
      strain,
At length he reads the *Golden Legend* clear,
  At length the *Lost Chord* finds itself again.

CECIL JOHN RHODES.

BORN 1853.   DIED MARCH 26, 1902.

Lo, while the dawn of every heart's desires,
    Herald of Peace, comes up the sombre sky,
Paling the night's wide ring of smouldering
    fires—
        He was ordained to die !

His work was Peace, though such should needs
    be wrought
    Only of hideous War's informing breath ;
And now another Peace than that he sought
        Is his by grace of Death.

Judgment is stayed ; so large he seems to loom
    Upon the moment's too immediate sight ;
The years that lie within the future's womb
        Shall weigh his worth aright.

This much we know, that through the shifting
    scenes,
    Triumph or ill-report, his end the same,
He strove to compass, by whatever means,
        The patriot's single aim.

His was the great heart hid in homely guise,
  His the imaginative force that reads
The fate of nations clear as other eyes
        Foretell to-morrow's needs.

He played with half a continent for stake,
  Unmoved alike by present praise or scorn,
Scheming his sanguine projects for the sake
        Of peoples yet unborn.

To stretch the bounds of Empire broader still,
  To make at last two kindred peoples one—
Such was the labour which, for good or ill,
        Dying he left undone.

Time may complete or mar the work he planned ;
  Himself, beyond the care of earthly fame—
The mountains guard him sleeping in the land
        To which he gave his name.

POPE LEO THE THIRTEENTH.

BORN 1810.   DIED JULY 20, 1903.

THERE in the hushed Cathedral's holy calm,
　　Dim lights about him, and the dome above,
He sleeps—immortal by the spirit-balm
　　　　Of universal love.

Still over lips and brow where life has passed
　　Lingers the smile of faith serenely fair ;
The hands that blessed the world are folded fast
　　　　As in the act of prayer.

The long day closes and the strife is dumb.
　　Thither he goes where temporal power is vain,
Where he that asks to enter must become
　　　　A little child again.

And, since in perfect humbleness of heart
　　He sought his Church's honour, not his own,
All faiths are one to share the mourner's part
　　　　Beside the empty throne.

High Guardian of the mysteries of God,
　　His circling love enwrapped the human race ;
For every creed the Pontiff's lifted rod
　　　　Blossomed with flowers of grace.

The nations' peace he had for dearest cause;
　Kings from his counsel caught a starry sign;
Christlike he fostered loyalty to laws,
　　　　　These earthly, those divine.

So shall the heart of grief not soon be cold,
　There least, where loyal tributes crown the
　　　way
Of Ireland's King whose hand, as friends may
　　　hold,
　　　　　He held but yesterday.

BRADBURY, AGNEW, AND CO. LD., LONDON AND TONBRIDGE.

A HARVEST OF CHAFF.